New England Year

NEW ENGLAND YEAR

A Journal of Vermont Farm Life

by Muriel Follett

Wood Engravings by Herbert Waters

YANKEE BOOKS

A division of Yankee Publishing Incorporated
Dublin, New Hampshire

Dedicated in loving memory to Rob,
the leading man in this book,
and to members of my family
for their loyal support.

New England Year was originally published in 1940 by
The Stephen Daye Press of Brattleboro, Vermont.

Designed by Jill Shaffer

Yankee Publishing Incorporated
Dublin, New Hampshire

First Yankee Books Edition

Library of Congress Cataloging-in-Publication Data

Follett, Muriel.
    New England year: a journal of Vermont farm life/by Muriel
Follett; wood engravings by Herbert Waters. — 2nd ed.
        p.   cm. — (A Yankee classic)
    Reprint. Originally published: Brattleboro, Vt.: Stephen Daye
Press, c1939.
    ISBN 0-89909-175-X : $14.95
    1. Vermont — Social life and customs. 2. Country life —
Vermont. 3. Farm life — Vermont. 4. Follett, Muriel — Diaries.
I. Waters, Herbert. II. Title. III. Series.
F54.F65 1988
974.3 — dc 19

JANUARY

SATURDAY, *January 1. Snow, followed by rain and sleet.* This is a nice day to sit by the fire and read. Snow and rain outside and a warm, sizzling wood fire in the house. There is a welcome let-down feeling after the fun and gaiety of the holiday season.

Bobby, who is twelve, sits in the big grandfather's chair by the stove, reading a new copy of *Treasure Island,* his brown eyes intent upon the pages and his light hair tousled. His ten-year-old sister, Jean, is curled up on the couch in the corner reading another Christmas book, *Heidi Grows Up.* It is not a good position for anyone's eyes, so I interrupt her reading and ask her to sit up straighter. She stretches like a contented kitten, sits up for a few minutes and then, as she gets immersed in the story again, slumps into the old position. She looks too happy to bother again so I let her alone and gaze dreamily out of the window at the snow on the ground, the gray sleet falling. The children's father, Rob, is coming down from the barn. I watch him as he stops by the snow house the children have built on

5

the little hill beside our house. He bends down to look in the open door; and I know, even from the distance, how high his color is in this weather, and the alert quiet interest in his eyes.

The children have lived all their lives on this hilltop farm in southeastern Vermont. They are the sixth generation in direct line to call this home. Their father and grandfather were born here. They love the high, rolling land, the woods and the fields, the big house and barns. It is all part of them.

The house looks as if it sat on top of the topmost hill as one sees it from the foot of the last hill below, after the climb up the winding road from the main thoroughfare, a mile away. The road follows a little meandering brook until it reaches the hairpin turn at the foot of Popl' Tree Hill and then branches out for itself, up by gnarled old apple trees and tall Lombardy poplars. And there, as the top of the hill is reached and the last corner turned, is the big white house built in a simple Colonial style in the year 1800. Back of it, on a slight hill, is the long red barn of more recent vintage. And all around are higher hills, pyramiding toward the sky, with narrow valleys between.

There is always color in the hills, color beside the dun brown of most vegetation in winter. And it is never the same from one season to the next. In winter, the evergreen pines and spruce and hemlocks make brave splashes of green among the leafless trees. White birches lose their virgin whiteness against the spotless snow of the highlands. But as the snow melts away in the spring, the same birch trees look silver white and their branches show feathery and green before other trees dare to flaunt their leaves. Summer brings masses of green, laced with blossoms, but autumn in Vermont turns the same hills to flaming splendor in reds, golds, and browns. People stare at our hills in amazement and then return again and again to look some more, fearing that their imaginations might have been playing tricks. But it is always more lovely than they had imagined.

When Vermont was young, the country road leading past our house was the main Boston Post Road from Boston to points north, and the house was a tavern where travelers could stop for a night — or a week — and find refreshment and rest. There is still in the house the window at the top of the stairs that used to open into the bar room, where the hard-drinking people of that day stopped on their way to the dance hall to fill up on hot, stinging potato whiskey, the whiskey that was made at the foot of Popl' Tree Hill not more than two stones' throw away.

There is in the house, also, the old fiddler's bench built over the stair well, with its two steps up and the low swinging door to shut the fiddlers away from the noisy, boisterous crowd of dancers. Hard, straight benches were nailed around the walls of the dance hall for the dancers to sit upon between the "square figures." Now those benches are gone and the long dance hall with the fireplace at one end has been divided to make two bedrooms.

The house still holds its quiet dignity, and its simple architecture fits well into our Vermont hills. It is big, rambling, rather inconvenient and far too large for the needs of one small family, with its fifteen rooms. The barn is comparatively modern, with concrete floors and steel stanchions for the cattle. The original barns were strung, in the old New England manner, one against another across the road from the house. The children's grandfather built the new barn toward the rear of the house and far enough away from it to leave a clear view of the valleys below, stretching away to the front and side of the house.

It's queer, I thought this was such a lonely spot when I first came to the old farm as a bride. I'll never forget how quiet and desolate everything seemed that first winter. Now I love it. But since then I have become acquainted with my neighbors, we have electricity instead of the old oil lamps, a radio, and the important labor saving devices.

Home is where one's roots are, I guess — and solitude is a blessing when one learns how to use it.

Monday, January 3. Rob has a job drawing ten cords of wood with the horses for Wade Brooks. The wood is all cut in the woods about two and a half miles from home. He had to draw it to Townshend village, two and a half miles in another direction. Most of his time is taken by traveling back and forth with the horses.

Mr. Brooks came up to the farm from his home in the village to help Rob lift the wide wooden bunks onto the sled. Rob drove the sled into the woods without any difficulty. It went well over the deep snow while it was empty. But when it was loaded with wood that was a different matter. The sled runners caught on stones and rocks hidden by the snow. The wide bunks hit against the nearby trees and stuck there. He finally had to unload the wood and take off the bunks.

He came home after the dray, a simple frame made for carrying wood, built from two long poles with the bark left on, and bolted to two cross pieces of wood about four feet in length, so the poles form a rack for wood to be piled upon which is slightly narrower than the front section of the sled. The dray is bolted to the short sled, and the smaller ends of the poles drag behind on the ground. It is much easier to get around in the woods with an outfit like that, but it can't be used much on a public road.

The dray worked well coming out of the woods. Rob started down the last steep hill which led to the main road. Suddenly the sled stopped with a jerk, pulling the horses, Nip and Tuck, back sharply onto their haunches. He located the trouble. One of the steel shoes on the sled runners had broken in two and one end was jammed into the ground for nearly two feet. That finished his work in the woods until he could get another sled assembled. He decided that the best thing to do was to build another sled, made entirely from new logs.

"While I'm about it," he said, "I had better build a sled that will stand the racket."

He cut and drew big logs from our own woods, cut from ash,

8

oak, and maple trees. He drew them down to the saw mill at the southern end of town in his father's truck, after they had been snaked out of the woods by the horses. They were sawed into the right sizes for the different sled pieces; one piece of oak for a pole, two lengths of maple for runners, and ash for the forward bunks. He used heavy iron shoes that he already had for sled runners, and the brace irons were taken from the old sled, since they were still strong and well made.

Wade Brooks and Mr. Lawrence, the local blacksmith, did most of the work of putting the sled together. It took longer than Rob expected.

Thursday, January 6. Rob went down to the village early this morning to get the sled. He brought it home fastened to the rear of our automobile. The runners skidded over the snow faster than they probably ever will again when drawn by horses.

The horses, Nip and Tuck, more commonly called Nipper and Sister, are twin black Percherons. Twin horses are quite rare. Nipper has a long white streak down the middle of his forehead, and Sister has a small round coin-like white mark on her face which just missed looking like a star. In a sense they are members of our family.

Friday, January 7. Rob began today getting his maple products ready for the Vermont State Farm Products Show in Burlington. It begins next week, the eleventh of January, and lasts through the fourteenth, so it means using last spring's syrup. He wants to enter all classes this year and it takes much time and preparation. (He won first prize in the state on his syrup last year.) He has been making soft pail sugar tonight. It seems just the right consistency — delicious, light, and fine enough so that the little grains dissolve almost as quickly as you can touch your tongue to them — but Rob is never quite satisfied. He is always hoping to get it just a little better.

9

He has to work on the maple products nights, he thinks, because he wants to get the wood drawn as soon as possible. He drew a little over two cords today.

Saturday, January 8. The maple entries are all done and ready to be shipped to Burlington, the soft pail sugar, the cake sugar, maple syrup, maple cream, cakes in pound boxes, and maple leaf candies which are put in fancy pound boxes wrapped in cellophane. It took nearly all day to get them finished.

Monday, January 10. The monthly meeting of the directors of the Cooperative Milk Plant at Brattleboro was held today. Rob is one of the seven directors. I went with him to Brattleboro.

Bobby has been saving his money for a new sled and with his Christmas money he had enough for the one he wanted. He gave me the money and drew a description of the kind of sled he wanted, the new kind with streamlines, the front an oval metal bar of the same material used for handlebars on bicycles.

I found it at Roberts' Hardware, and he loves it. Jean already has a good sled which Bobby painted for her so it looks like new.

We have a number of good sliding places in the mowings around our house, so the children don't have to slide in the road. There is a fair crust on the snow since the storm ten days ago and the youngsters make the most of it. They go out bundled to the ears and come back after the exertion of climbing hills, with their jackets unbuttoned and their cheeks rosy. I like to go sliding with them and they take turns lending me their sleds. I still slide down the hill lying on my tummy on the sled, with my feet acting as rudders or brakes behind. And Bobby and Jean help me with my tasks in the house so I can go with them more often. They are getting big so fast that I want to have all the time possible with them before they grow up and are gone.

Both children have dark eyes like their Dad's, and light hair.

They have both passed the chubby stage and are fast approaching the slim, leggy age. Jean is quieter than her more loquacious brother — but to me they are equally interesting. If I tried I couldn't decide which age they have passed through is the most to be enjoyed.

Tuesday, January 11. Rob went over to the Morgan Horse Farm today to help our neighbor, Royal, thresh his oats. The farmers around here often exchange work, which helps everyone.

He came home full of dust and his eyes were rimmed with it where his glasses came. The usual high color in his face was grayed until his head looked like a mask. The weather was cold and crisp so he didn't mind the dust as much as sometimes. The men had trouble with the belt that runs from the tractor to the threshing machine, so they couldn't finish the oats today. Rob hopes they will get done by noon tomorrow. Threshing is an inside job, usually done in the winter in this section of Vermont.

Wednesday, January 12. Rob went over to Royal's this morning as soon as the chores were done. He has fourteen cows to milk. The milk has to be taken down to the main road a mile away, where it is shipped in trucks to the milk plant in Brattleboro.

The threshing wasn't finished until afternoon so Caroline, Royal's wife, had the gang of six or seven extra men to dinner for the second day.

Rob is already starting to think of maple sugaring time, which usually begins around the middle of March. Before that time he hopes to cut about thirty cords of wood, to be used for next winter's supply at the house, and for firing the arch under the evaporator during sugaring. He also wants to get out several thousand feet of logs before that time, to be sawed into boards for use on the farm.

Thursday, January 13. Rob started for the woods early this morning to draw some more wood for Wade Brooks. He can only draw two loads of wood a day no matter how early he starts, because it takes so long to get there and back again. He rose at four-thirty this morning and finished chores at ten o'clock tonight. We will have to get a hired man right away.

My mother spent the afternoon with me. She lives just a mile away. While she was gone from home, Jed Hill, a neighbor who is staying with them this winter, shut off the cold water faucet in the kitchen sink and forgot to turn it on again. It froze solid. They are trying desperately to get it started again. If they don't, it means carrying water all the rest of the winter from the spring across the road from their house. Simple carelessness can be criminal in the country!

We were given a beautiful star-pattern patchwork quilt for Christmas by Rob's aunts who live in Weston. On the card which accompanied it was written: "This quilt was pieced by Robert's great-grandmother, Abigail (Johnson) Kimball, some time before the 'gay nineties.' We thought you might like it."

I adore it. I was torn between wanting to preserve it carefully by putting it away, upstairs, and wanting to enjoy it right now. I decided to enjoy it now. It is now on my bed where I am constantly finding new and pretty quilt blocks to admire.

My baby bassinet was taken down to Hazel's today. Jed Hill took it down on the back of his car. Hazel is a friend of ours and her baby girl is two weeks old today.

The bassinet, which is now shorn and sanitary, has quite a history. Rob and his two brothers slept in it when they were tiny. At that time it was draped with lace and ribbons and muslin. Rob's mother told me the names of all the *boy* babies in town who used it, but I don't remember them all. There were fifteen or sixteen. Then my Bobby had it, and Jean. Then my brother's two girls, then Hazel's oldest child, then Sonny Aither and now Hazel's new baby, Priscilla. It is still going strong. The "gingerbread" is gone and it looks simply like a clothes basket on standards, painted white. It is easily cleaned, and brightened by the pretty blankets within.

Sunday, January 16. It's a beautiful winter day today; sunny and not too cold. Rob doesn't have to take the milk Sunday mornings during the winter, so we can sleep late. I like to wake up slowly and peacefully, with no insistent br-r-ring of the alarm clock which shatters the early morning darkness of week-day mornings, when Rob jumps hurriedly out of bed to choke the thing into silence.

We dallied along this morning and didn't have breakfast until nine o'clock. Rob wouldn't eat until the cows were milked. Then he hustled through his chores so we could have most of the day together.

We went for a ride in the late afternoon, just the four of us. The children enjoy the foursome as much as we do. . . . They call our attention to the slopes that are good for sliding or to the snow-laden birches that make good swings. In return we point out to them the upper wood-road where the sled-marks mean that Father has started hauling from his woodlot. . . . Our children seem to understand the importance of both signs.

On the way home we stopped at Mother's and Father's. . . . Rob's own mother died a number of years ago, and two years later my father died. Later my mother married Rob's father and they live about a mile from our home. It makes some interesting relationships, since my mother is also my mother-in-law, and my husband my step-brother! The children's paternal and maternal grandparents are one and the same family.

Rob started his chores early so we could have a long evening together. Before he had finished, Jed Hill came in, looking rather disheveled and vaguely uneasy. He is tall, rangy, with light brown hair and pale blue eyes, and inclined to be lazy. He asked if he could use our telephone.

I wondered at his long telephone conversations, but I didn't hear anything he said for the radio was going strong. Finally, when Rob came in from the barn, Jed told us that he had taken Mother's car to come up here and had run it over the bank and into the brook beside the road. Jed had been calling for the wrecker to come and get it out, and the nearest one was in Newfane.

Rob told him that getting the wrecker up here in the evening would cost a small fortune and that he would help get the car out of the brook. Royal, our good neighbor, came over and helped. But it was one o'clock in the morning before the car was finally hauled out, apparently unhurt, and Rob and Royal could get home.

I was furious. Why couldn't Jed have stayed home? And Rob was exhausted. He has to get up before five in the morning, while Jed can sleep until noon if he wants to; he hasn't much to do. . . . And I was lonesome too.

It has started to snow again.

Monday, January 17. The children hated to go to school today because of the sleety weather but the school bus made it all right.

When they got home tonight Bobby acted quite disgusted. He came stalking into the living room with his windbreaker still on and his overshoes dripping snow.

"Mother," he said, "Mother, do you know what? I didn't have any recess today." He was terribly disgruntled. "All the other kids had their recess but Ruthy and me."

"What was the matter?" I asked.

"Oh, gosh, we had to practice a song to sing together."

"What was so awful about that?"

"We-ll," and that was all he said for a while. Then, "Mother, you know that song I told you about? It's awful! It's a loving song."

Tuesday, January 18. Fair, very cold. Twelve below zero. When the children got home from school tonight Bobby rushed into the house and shouted,

"Mother, I don't have to sing that song. I joined the harmonica class and the teacher said that anyone who belonged to the

15

harmonica class couldn't be in anything else. I'm awfully glad. So is Ruthy."

Later in the evening he remarked out of a silence,

"That song really was pretty. I really liked the music. But Ruthy is glad we don't have to sing it."

Jean had to write a poem in school today. She was unable to think of a subject and the teacher suggested that she write about, "My Brother." Jean wrote:

> My brother is so funny
> It's quite disgusting.

She told Bobby about it and he immediately composed one entitled, "My Sister."

> My shrimp sister is a girl
> I'm going to take her for a whirl.
> She is a loud-mouthed baboon
> Ha, ha, ha, ha
> She always says bah.
> She hasn't grown up
> For she's just a little pup.

That started them both off into lots of nonsense. When they came home they bandied rhymes back and forth at each other until they went to bed. And even then we heard them shouting ditties from their bedrooms until they became drowsy.

Wednesday, January 19. Cold. Twenty degrees below zero. Clear. Thank goodness the wind is not blowing. We would freeze if it did.

Bobby stayed home from school today. I haven't decided whether he is really ill — or bluffing. Possibly both.

Last night when he got home from school he complained of a stomach-ache, so he didn't have to do his usual chores at the barn. His favorite radio stories begin at five in the afternoon. Could that have anything to do with it? He said he felt better

16

this morning but not well enough to go to school. He wrote letters most of the morning and his appetite was singularly unimpaired. I made him take a long nap this afternoon. Along about three-thirty he said,

"Do you think I *ought* to go out doors today?"

I bit, absent-mindedly.

"You'd better stay rather quiet," I told him.

His father came in about four o'clock and asked, "Are you going to help me with the chores tonight, Bobby?"

"Mother said I ought not to go out," Bobby said.

Rob looked at me inquiringly. I told him what I had said and added,

"It's too bad he doesn't feel better. Maybe I'd better put him right to bed before his stories."

Bobby said he felt better immediately and he rushed up to the barn to get his chores done quickly. His father said he *acted* all right, the way he flew about. He didn't mention feeling ill again and he ate two helpings of everything for dinner.

I wonder. . . .

Saturday, January 22. Several inches of snow fell last night and this morning all the trees and branches and shrubbery are ribbed inch deep. It looks like an old Currier and Ives print around here with the red barn standing out in bold relief against the snow. It makes one want to get out doors and fling around in it and blow it about like feathers.

Several automobiles have been stuck on the curve at the foot of Popl' Tree Hill and Rob has had to help most of them to get out. Long experience with that turn has made him very efficient in navigating it. The drivers of the cars look very sheepish when he backs their cars out of the snowbanks they have driven into and drives them up the hill without any trouble. He says it's all in knowing how.

Sunday, January 23. Clear, comparatively warm. A beautiful day. Three hunters from Dover came this afternoon with their guns and snowshoes. They asked permission to hunt bobcats on our land. Rob knew the father of one of the hunters, he said, so he thought they were all right and he gave them permission. All our land is posted.

Royal killed a bobcat in a trap last Sunday. There is a five dollar bounty on the animals.

The snowplow came through late this afternoon and went back about eight o'clock this evening. The roads ought to be good now.

Monday, January 24. Warm. Fair in the morning and rain in the late afternoon and evening. Wash day. Enough said. Rob fixed a nice clothesline from the corner of the house to the big maple tree by the barn. The line runs on a pulley. I think maybe he hopes that he won't have to shovel any more snow from under the clotheslines.

When the children came home from school tonight Bobby told me that he and Ruthy had been persuaded to sing the Courting Song as a duet. Bobby sang it to me, pausing for blushes. The tune is very pretty and the words are more suggestive of courting than actually spoken.

Tuesday, January 25. It rained hard all night and the wind blew strongly from the south. I'm glad it wasn't all snow.

Rob took the children down to Mother's, near the main road, when he took the milk this morning. He didn't think the school bus could get up the hill. That meant some hustling around to get them ready by seven-thirty, when the milk had to go.

Stanley Martin walked over with his shovel from his home a mile-and-a-half over the hill. He turned the water out of the road with his shovel as he came along. He went on down toward Mother's, where there were some pretty bad spots in places. The culverts were all full and water was running over into the road. Snow is melting fast. I heard that the ice had gone out of the West River.

We sent sixteen quarts of milk to school today for the hot lunches. Parents take turns sending food there.

Wednesday, January 26. Colder. Snow flurries. Rob killed our pig today. Jed Hill came to help. Rob didn't weigh the pig but he estimated the weight at three hundred pounds.

Late this afternoon, after the body heat was gone, he brought the pig down from the barn and into the kitchen to cut it up. We put an old table in the center of the kitchen, spread newspapers on it and then an oilcloth. The pig was halved on it and became two large slabs of pork.

Jean looked at the pork and wanted to know, "What part does the sausage come from?"

I was in a hurry and I answered briefly, "The waste." I meant the small pieces of good meat which might otherwise go to waste.

"The waist?" she repeated. "Where is a pig's waist?"

I couldn't tell her.

Rob spent the evening cutting the pork into hams and bacon, chops and strips for salt pork and sausage and lard. We have to wait twenty-four hours, or until the pork is thoroughly cool, before we begin the process of curing it. In the meantime, two tables in the kitchen are literally overflowing with pork so we can hardly move without hitting it.

The radio news items tonight told of snow in Florida and a terrible ice jam at Niagara Falls. One power plant on the Canadian side of the Falls has already been abandoned and the one on the United States side cut down. The bridge is buckling in the middle. Crowds pack the banks on both sides. It must be an awe-inspiring sight!

Thursday, January 27. Fair, cold. Looked like a storm toward night. The bridge across Niagara Falls went out today. Workmen tried to save it until about ten minutes before it collapsed.

19

We have been thinking pork and breathing pork and eating pork all day today. We enjoyed it the first hour but all of us felt slightly nauseated before night.

The fat pork was "tried out" to make lard. It had to be cubed in small pieces first and then put on the stove in large kettles and pans so the lard could melt, leaving the "crackles." Then the lard was strained and put in pails to keep. The smoky, penetrating odor went all over the house.

We left the table in the middle of the kitchen tonight, with one end propped up to let some of the meat drain. We are processing it for ham and bacon. The meat has had its first rubbing of smoke salt.

Rob helped us cut the meat most of the day. We talked of pickling the pig's feet but decided against it. He convulsed us all when he pretended to fasten the pig's ears to his own head and asked us if we didn't think it an improvement in his looks. Only he turned the ears on end so they stuck up straight, the points coming above the top of his head — like Puck.

We are all very tired tonight. Rob fell asleep in his chair beside the stove and I had a hard time waking him.

Friday, January 28. Clear and cold. This evening Rob took me down to Newfane to a meeting of the Health Councils of Townshend and Newfane. We are planning a big Health Institute in May with several state speakers — specialists in their line of health work. The state workers had a letter from Governor Aiken commending the program. He may be one of the speakers. All the teachers and town officials in the county are to be invited. We hope they will become more health-conscious, and thus reach all the people in the towns.

Our minister plans to leave for his new pastorate right away. We shall miss him and his family. He has done a lot of health work in Townshend.

We haven't a new minister yet, but a retired minister in

Newfane plans to supply the pulpit (what a queer phrase, *supply the pulpit*) until we get another one.

Saturday, January 29. Clear, slightly warmer. Jed Hill helped Rob cut wood today and was here for dinner. Bobby helped the men in the woods during the morning. He hated the idea at first and thought it was terrible to have to help chop wood. But this noon he said he enjoyed chopping, and helping on one end of the cross-cut saw.

Ruth, the girl who helps me around the house, left tonight for the week-end. She has every other week-end off. She had a sick headache in the morning and felt miserable. I tried to make her lie down and rest but she said that if she wasn't able to do her work she wouldn't have the nerve to go away and have a good time afterward. She did a lot of cooking to leave for us.

June Brown came to see Jean this afternoon. They played hospital, with Bobby as the doctor for a while, and then went sliding in the big mowing in front of the house.

Sunday, January 30. A beautiful day, sunny and not very cold. Bobby and Jean got up early this morning before the rest of us were stirring. Bobby went to the barn and milked four or five cows and watered and fed the horses.

Jean made pancakes for breakfast all by herself. She decided the recipe didn't make enough so she doubled it. The pancakes were delicious, light and tender. I don't believe I could have done that all by myself when I was ten years old. She helped me with the housework too, and it was all done in almost no time.

We had a lazy, enjoyable day, just the four of us. We went out doors and roamed around, and then came in again to sit by the fire and read. We want the children to know that quiet and solitude can be as enjoyable as noise and action — and that it helps re-stock their vitality.

FEBRUARY

T UESDAY, *February 1. Clear, cold and windy. About zero.* This
has been such a beautiful day. Rob had to go to Brattleboro after grain this morning, so I went with him.
There is no heater in the truck so I put on my ski pants to keep
warm.

I finished my light blue wool dress this afternoon and Ruth
pressed it beautifully. I wore it to the Parent-Teachers Association supper at the town hall this evening.

Many of the people at the supper wore costumes of forty and
fifty years ago. I had none ready or I would have worn one too.
Some were very lovely but clothes certainly fit better today!

The school music teacher topped the old style attractions
with a costume fearfully and wonderfully put together. The
black hat she wore sat high on her head. It was decorated with
an enormous hatpin, its head a maze of brilliants, and three
ostrich plumes of various colors and sizes which waved and
fluttered when she talked in her energetic way. Her dress
combined a rose-colored underskirt which had been in her

22

mother's trousseau, an overskirt of black with handmade three-inch fringe around the bottom, and a black waist puffed in the most unusual places and topped by a fichu of white, hand-embroidered lace made by her grandmother. Worn by Miss Ackers, with her cocky, bird-like manner, the entire costume was too delightful for words.

Bobby and Ruthy sang their Courting Song duet, dressed in quaint old costumes.

Wednesday, February 2. Slightly warmer. Clear in morning and cloudy toward evening. One of the town officers called today about the possibilities of fixing the town hall kitchen. Some of the men have fought against the idea, but he said that he went into the kitchen last night while the women were working there and he never realized before just how small the kitchen was. (He might have added, nor how large most of the women who worked there.) He suggested that if the women could organize and decide just what they wanted done, maybe something could be voted upon at Town Meeting next month. But that is the difficulty.

It is plain to see that a man designed the kitchen with no understanding of the problems we women face when preparing a public dinner, serving it, and cleaning up afterward. With just one partition removed and the cupboards rearranged, and possibly another sink added, the kitchen would be much more convenient. Then the working centers — tables, and so forth — could be moved to better positions. But the women have been unable to agree upon anything, definitely. There seem to be too many good suggestions. We will have to try to get together on the plans this month.

Rob and his father started to fill Father's ice house today. Father has a nice little pond not far from his house, which makes ice cutting handy. Rob plans to fill our ice house as soon as enough snow comes to make the roads slippery enough for sleds, so the horses can easily draw the loads of heavy ice.

The thaw last week took off most of the snow. The roads, and even the tops of the surrounding hills, are bare. The places where the ground is still covered are icy — regular skating rinks, although some are perpendicular!

Thursday, February 3. Light rain changing to snow and sleet. I woke up this morning after a terrible dream. I dreamed that Rob was dead and I was wandering around, lost without him. What a relief it was when I reached over and felt him still beside me. I turned over and pressed against him for a long time before I felt sure he was really there, and before I could stop trembling. He woke up enough to reassure me.

He has been having a hard cold on his lungs and I have been worrying about him. That probably accounts for my terrible dream. I wish he would stay in bed so he could get over it.

Ruth and I made the sausage this morning. We have a regular sausage grinder that turns with a hand crank, and we made twenty-one pounds of sausage. We left it in a big kettle until after we had fried some and sampled it at dinner tonight, so everyone could have a chance to comment on the flavor and decide if it needed more seasoning, more pepper, sage, ginger or cloves. Everyone was satisfied, so we stuffed most of it into cloth casings after the dishes were done tonight. When the sausage is thoroughly chilled, the casings will be coated with paraffin to keep it fresh. I'm going to can some tomorrow in the pressure cooker.

Friday, February 4. Warmer, partly cloudy. Rob's cold was heavier today and I managed to persuade him to stay in while I applied mustard plasters. I'd tried everything else the doctor advocated without results, and even the hot skunks' oil which his father insisted upon. He felt a little better tonight and went out to the barn to do his chores, although he shouldn't. Rob is scornful of human frailty!

Mother called on the telephone while we were eating supper to ask about Rob. Bobby answered the telephone.

"Oh, he's all right except he's a little tight in his —" long pause "— well, he's a little *tight,* that's all."

The rest of us were convulsed.

"What's the matter?" Bobby wanted to know. "I didn't know *where* he was tight and I had to say *something,* didn't I?"

Today has been a day composed of little tasks — mending clothes, putting them away, reading. It has been quiet, but all too short. I went out into the open shed this afternoon and stood in the doorway, breathing the good-tasting, fresh-smelling cold air. I wanted to go for a long walk, but the paths and roads are so icy after yesterday's snow and sleet that walking is dangerous. We have wood ashes sprinkled on all the paths from the house to the barn.

Jean brought home a book from the library tonight. It's *Five Little Peppers and How They Grew.* She persuaded Ruth to leave tonight's dishes until tomorrow morning so she could read more this evening. One of her tasks is to help with the dishes. She even left part of her fresh hot rolls and maple syrup so she could start reading sooner and then her hard-hearted mother made her help clear the table and put away the food.

Monday, February 7. Warm and sunny. Forty-four degrees. Bobby and Jean awoke before I did this morning. They came back upstairs and woke me up. Ruth had told them that Larry, a boy in Bobby's room at school, died yesterday. It doesn't seem possible. Larry was one of Bobby's best friends, about a year older. (Larry went to school last Friday morning and died early Sunday with pneumonia.) The children are all broken up about it.

Bobby said, "Larry was always so generous. He let me ride his bicycle 'most any time." Then, "Larry was always good to the little kids. He looked out for them. . . . Larry was one of my best friends." Then, over and over, "It *can't* be true about *Larry.*

I can't believe it; it *couldn't* happen so quick." Then, later, "Do you suppose I would die as quick as that?"

Bobby took a quarter from his own money to buy flowers for Larry. He is going to see that the school children send flowers. I hope the children aren't expected to attend the funeral. That would be tragic for all of them. . . .

Ruth went to church yesterday. Mr. Haynes from Newfane preached. She said there was a beautiful begonia on the corner of the pulpit. It was in a nice jardiniere and the whole thing looked lovely. When the minister started his prayer he leaned his hands on the edge of the pulpit. Suddenly a board lifted on the top of the pulpit, enough to jar the plant. It fell crashing to the floor. The minister prayed on.

John Jones, from West Townshend, came last night to work for Rob. He appears to be a nice lad, about seventeen years old. He is six feet three inches tall and carries himself like a soldier; straight, with broad shoulders squared. He wasn't sure whether he wanted to work or not but his father suggested that he try it for a week anyway, so that is what he is doing. I hope he will work out well.

Rob's cold is a little better.

I like to see clean clothes blowing on the line. Ours were out early this morning. The clothes danced and swayed as they haven't done before in months. It won't be long now before spring comes.

I wish I could paint a word picture of the beauty of the bare branches of the maple tree outside the dining room window, against the vivid blue winter sky. The delicate tracery of the dull silver branches, the swift white clouds scuttling across the bright inverted bowl make ever-changing patterns. Words are so heavy for anything so graceful.

Tuesday, February 8. Cold and sunny. The man who tests the milk came last night. Not the regular man but a substitute. The regular tester is sick with the mumps. I didn't know where to

27

have him sleep, for our five bedrooms are all occupied. Finally, I decided to let him have Bobby's room, and I put a cot in my room for Bobby.

Jean woke up this morning feeling sick. She didn't feel well enough to go to school but she improved rapidly during the morning after the school bus left. The funeral for their friend, Larry, is this afternoon and the school children are expected to go. It has affected her very deeply, as it has all the children.

Rob and his father have been trying to saw wood today. (John is about sick with a cold in his head and has been staying in the house all day.) Rob had a hard time trying to start his tractor. It was so stiff that he couldn't turn it over with the crank, so the men pushed it out of the barn and down the incline toward the house. Then they built a small fire under it to warm it up. The wind was so strong it blew the blaze up against the tractor and the gas in the carburetor caught fire. They managed to put it out before any damage was done, and after the thing was warmed up, it started all right. They sawed several cords of wood before they had to stop for chores.

Royal came over a few evenings ago and he and Rob discussed making sleds for sugaring. The lightest and toughest wood around here is ash. They discussed the size and length of the logs needed for sled runners. During sugaring, the snow often melts away in the woods and leaves deep mud behind. A steel-shod sled is all right on snow, but it squeaks and sticks on mud, and horses can't draw such a sled loaded with several barrels of sap, so wood-shod sleds are used. Of course the wood runners wear through in time, but they slip over the muddy wood roads fairly easily. Now, as everyone knows, the front of the sled runners curve up. All the oldtimers agree that the strongest and best runners are made by the trees themselves. So the men have been looking through the woods for ash trees with crooks in their limbs or trunks, to make the proper curve for sled runners. Royal has found one or two trees with good crooks and Rob knows where there is one in the woods, only it

28

isn't large enough yet. It needs to grow several years more. Ash trees with growing sled crooks are hard to find.

The alternative is to make wooden runners in two pieces, with a long splice at the junction. The men have been discussing the proper way to splice the runners, but that is a subject for experts.

Our driveway is full of ice now, although the roads are nearly bare. Rob predicts that we will have a storm soon.

Friday, February 11. Partly cloudy and cold. Below zero in the morning. I went with Rob to Brattleboro yesterday when he went to his milk plant meeting, and picked out several patterns for clothes I'm planning to make this spring: a dress pattern and a playsuit pattern for Jean and coat and dress patterns for me. I'll have to get a coat pattern for Jean later if I find the right material.

While I was shopping in Woolworth's, I met the Kepps of Jamaica. Mr. and Mrs. Kepp were taking Leone, their youngest daughter, out of business school because of her health. The whole family, including Leone's older sister, Sara, were noticeably worried. They expected that Leone might eventually need an operation.

I told Mrs. Kepp that operations weren't so bad, that I had spent three weeks in a hospital for an operation not so long ago, and that I had managed to have quite a good time. Mrs. Kepp raised her voice — which usually carries very well indeed — and called across the large store to Leone.

"Leone, come over here."

While Leone was coming over, Mrs. Kepp turned to her older daughter, standing by her side, and said,

"Muriel said she just spent three weeks in the hospital and she *never* had such a good time before."

She repeated it a minute later to Leone, with variations:

"Muriel said she just spent three weeks in the hospital and she had the best time she'd ever had in her life!"

Leone looked at me doubtfully, and I wondered what proportions the story would assume at the next telling . . . and the next.

This noon Rob took me to the village to a Home Demonstration meeting at Mrs. Rice's. We had what they call a one-dish meal, hot tamale pie. It was very good, with corn meal a substitute for potatoes or macaroni. And for dessert, prune and nut pudding with whipped cream. Altogether, I felt that the afternoon was very worthwhile. The next meeting is on "layettes". Quite appropriate for many young mothers in town, although for myself, I wished it could have come some twelve years earlier.

The women at the meeting took a vote on a resolution to remodel the town hall dining room, to be brought before Town Meeting next month. They were unanimous in wanting it done.

Saturday, February 12. The children spent the afternoon with the Sibleys. They, and a group of children from the neighborhood, planned to go up on the big hill back of Perry's and explore the caves which are up there. I am glad they were persuaded to wait until later, during the summertime. It is quite probable that the caves are inhabited by bears and foxes at this season of the year.

John's little nephew has pneumonia and John left here early to go home to see how he is.

Tuesday, February 15. Clear and cold. Rob feels a little better today. His cold is looser, thank Heaven. John came back yesterday morning. His nephew is no better.

Yesterday was a warm, windy day and the washing dried well. I am glad it is done for this week because today is so much colder. We ironed this morning.

This afternoon I went with Mr. and Mrs. Martin to Newfane to a County Health Unit Meeting where Dr. Clark of Burlington was the principal speaker, although other state and county health workers were present. They were really asking for money from the different towns in the county for child health work, and to help support the district nurse. Our unit is composed of eleven towns. If every town in the unit voted up to three per cent on the grand list for this work, it would be sufficient. Each dollar raised by towns for this work will be matched, dollar for dollar, by the federal government. There are nine similar units throughout the state of Vermont, and more will be formed when there is more money.

Nine towns were represented out of the eleven in our county. Many town officials were present. The people there felt that each town should try to raise the necessary money. I was asked to explain it at our Town Meeting in March.

Thursday, February 17. Yesterday and today I have sewed during nearly all my spare time. I didn't feel too ambitious (a little cold, I think) so I turned to sewing. I have two dresses for Jean all done but finishing the hems, and a blouse for myself. The cloth for one of Jean's dresses, a remnant, cost ten cents and my blouse will cost a quarter; fifteen cents for the remnant of blue lace and ten cents for rainbow buttons. Both pieces were nice and fine, but not large enough for bigger garments. Made up in a store they wouldn't sell for under a dollar apiece — maybe more. It's a big saving to sew for the family.

Rob and John have been drawing wood for the house and the sugar house. We were short of dry wood, so they have been cutting the dry lower limbs from pine trees in the woods. Rob shinnies up the trees, sometimes as high as fifteen feet from the ground, and cuts the dead limbs as he goes up. He says he doesn't recommend that practice, but that it works well in a pinch.

Friday, February 18. I am glad days like this don't happen often!
To begin with, I awoke early and started to think about some

letters that must go at once. I wrote them before breakfast so Rob could take them when he took the milk at seven-thirty.

I hadn't finished when Ruth said she was ill with the grippe and that her head ached so she couldn't stand up. She wanted to go home where her mother could care for her, because she might be ill for several days.

The roads are extremely slippery from last night's rain, which froze on, and Rob thought the school bus would be unable to make the hill. So the children and Ruth all went with Rob at seven-thirty. Well, I got them off, but it was rather hectic around here for a while, getting everyone ready.

Soon, John came in and stood in front of me without speaking. I looked up, and his face was all bloody.

"I got hurt," he said simply.

A stick of wood he was chopping had flown up and hit him squarely between his eyes. He was nearly out on his feet.

I cleaned the wound with disinfectant and washed away the blood. The cut ran across the top of his nose where his nose and forehead join. It wasn't very deep but it extended down to the corner of his left eye. Together, we managed to get his boots off and he went to bed for the rest of the day, while I kept busy putting cold compresses on his face. One eye was quite inflamed but it cleared up toward night. He insisted that he didn't want a doctor.

Rob came home about noon and he had had a headache all the morning which had grown increasingly worse. I persuaded him to rest during the afternoon until chore time and I rubbed his head until he fell asleep. What would I have done if Ruth had been here?

Fortunately, the youngsters held up well. They helped me get supper when they got home from school but by that time I was nearly exhausted myself.

A friend stopped in during the evening and he and Rob talked politics. That is the main topic of conversation in all the small towns in Vermont this time of year. They may forget about it more or less for the rest of the year but not before town meeting. People linger in stores and post-offices and all public buildings, as well as in their homes and discuss all the town affairs; especially the things they would like to see changed.

Saturday, February 19. Partly cloudy and warmer. We made out a long list this morning of things that must be done today, and the things to cook. Everything was finished by night except for mending a few stockings. Jean washed the kitchen, bathroom and pantry floors. She insisted upon doing it. And Bobby vacuumed around the house where it needed doing, although he hates the job. I made crab apple jelly from juice I canned last fall. It was a very satisfying day.

Sunday, February 20. Mostly fair and warm for this season in Vermont. We haven't done much but loaf today. I had plenty of food cooked, so that part was a cinch. The roads are still so icy we only navigate them when we need to, and others stay away.

I saw an advertisement in the *American Book Mart* asking for old books. It made us start hunting up our old books. They may not be valuable but their titles are interesting. One was *Gathered Sketches of New Hampshire and Vermont,* another, *A Treatiſe on Infant Baptiſm* with the old style "S" (written "on the ſeventeenth day of July in the thirty-ſecond year of the Independence of the United Statef of America).

There was also a *Sander's Reader,* 1853; an *Anti-Slavery Manual — Facts and Arguments on American Slavery,* 1839; and *Religion Recommended to Youth* by Caroline Matilda Thayer in 1847.

We heard from Ruth today. She didn't feel equal to coming back today but maybe tomorrow. . . .

John appeared with a new haircut tonight. Now his hair won't have a chance to reach his shoulders — and only an inch or so to go. He still has a patch across his nose, and a toothache. His little nephew who has pneumonia is better, but he may have to be taken to the hospital to have his lungs tapped.

Monday, February 21. Fair and warm. Today smells and feels like a shy advance toward spring. It is beautiful and warm with that special softness in the air. . . .

Rob and John spent the morning chopping wood over in the south lot. In the afternoon they went down to Father's pond and plowed out ice cakes with the ice plow. They plan to fill our ice house tomorrow.

We went down to the folks' tonight. We had a nice social evening with a few neighbors dropping in. It was late when we got home.

Tuesday, February 22. Cloudy and colder. Snow at night. Ruth came back last night. It is good having her here again. She feels fairly well again, although rather weak.

We did the washing in the morning.

Rob, Father, and Royal were filling the ice house all day. Father can bring up eighteen cakes of ice at a time (12 x 12 x 24), and Royal can load twenty-six cakes onto the wagon. Then, when the ice is up here it has to be packed away in the ice house, with layers of sawdust (and snow if they have it) between the layers of ice.

Two men are down on the ice pond all the time sawing out the cakes of ice. The cakes are plowed lengthwise first, with the ice plow drawn by horses. Then they are sawed the other way by hand with an ice saw. The ice is about twelve inches thick now.

There were seven for dinner this noon. Ruth learned how differently one needs to feed men doing heavy seasonal work like hauling ice, harvesting crops or filling silos. Men take lots of filling, for they get empty way down to their toes. They want to eat when they are ready; no waiting! They want the plates around at their places where they can begin dishing out food as soon as they've washed and can walk to their chairs. And they will begin at once, whether or not the food is all on the table, and woe betide the women who are not ready! From then on, there's not much use in the women sitting down at the table. As soon as one dish is filled, another is empty, and there is a continual shuffle back and forth from the kitchen stove to the dining table until the men are filled. It doesn't take long, twenty minutes or so, and the biggest dish won't stay filled. It is amazing how they stow away all that food. They want no fancy dish of salad, although cole slaw, or something similar, helps the rest of the food slide down more easily. And none of those silly desserts. Pie, and plenty of it, is good enough for them. They want a big kettle of coffee ready, with enough for two or three — or more — cups apiece. The pies are put on the table whole, and are slid off onto the same plates they began with. They can't stop for anything so silly as to have the plates changed. They can't stop for anything!

Ruth thought she had more than enough potatoes, but they were all gone in short order.

I'll never forget the first time I served a crew like that, when I was a green bride. Rob warned me to have plenty to eat, and I did, but he never told me how to set the table. I wanted to make a good impression on my new neighbors, so I got out my best linen and served the food à la Emily Post. I never tried it again! Shades of my ancestors, it was awful!

Wednesday, February 23. The men finished filling the ice house today — about 450 cakes. The weather turned warm last night and the ice started to melt before it could be packed away, but it didn't honeycomb.

I asked Father whether ice cut better in cold or warmer weather. He answered with his usual Yankee dryness, his nice, deep-set gray eyes twinkling and his mouth sober:

"Ice usually cuts best when you bear down on the saw."

Afterward, he said that during extremely cold weather the ice would stick to the saw unless it was kept moving briskly.

Saturday, February 26. Royal and his man helped Rob cut wood today and were here to dinner. That made eight of us. Bobby went to the woods this morning with the men and piled the wood they cut.

Ruth and I did a big baking this morning. While Ruth made sponge bread and rolls and three fruit pies, I made oatmeal macaroons and brownies.

This afternoon the four of us went for a walk down the hill toward the main road. Bobby lent me his new sled and I slid down across the big mowing. It is fun to forget one is grown up and go sliding "belly-bunt" down a long hill, using one's toes for brakes, with the wind whistling by one's ears. I know of no other sport which offers just that sort of thrill.

On the way home we stopped beside the road, where the little brook often overflows in times of high water. Some cranberries grow near the road on the boggy ground. We picked most of them last fall, but a few were left among the leaves and grasses. The snow had melted away from the spot today and we found a number of cranberries left, still looking firm and red and very edible. We picked them and put them in one of Jean's mittens and brought them home. Jean washed them and put them through the food chopper, with some raw apples, and added sugar. It was the best relish anyone ever tasted.

Sunday, February 27. Cold. Snow flurries. We finished our breakfast at ten o'clock this morning. Scandalous! We had tangerines, pancakes and maple syrup, home-grown sausages and milk and coffee. And we ate enough to last all day.

Rob wanted to go away this afternoon and he wanted to start early. None of us felt hungry at noon, so we had a light lunch. Bobby wanted to stay with his grandparents while Jean went with us.

We went to Windham where my great-aunt Hattie Jones and her son Paul Jones live. We had a fine time visiting with them and looking over the reports from towns in all sections of the state. Paul has a large collection of town reports and they are all interesting and informative.

The roads between Windham and Townshend are terribly rough and wash-boardy. We felt shaken to pieces before we got home. The road down Windham hill was slippery, too, and we skidded around plenty, coming down.

Anna and Roger Ela stopped this morning and told us they had promised their old Packard touring car to the town to use as a fire truck. It sounds like a good thing for the town, and we ought to have adequate fire protection of some sort.

Monday, February 28. Six below zero and the wind blowing a gale. This is one of the worst days of the winter. Rob got up early while I stayed in bed, snug under the covers until I felt ashamed of myself — but oh, so comfortable.

Rob came upstairs after he had taken the milk and remarked,

"It's six below zero and pretty 'owly out."

"Quite bilious weather," he added. "We wouldn't feel it so much if it wasn't for this cutting wind."

Only an inch of snow fell here last night, but it is light and dry and the wind whips it into high drifts, and then whips it out again with a swirl and a bellow. The wind *sounds* so cold as it moans around the house. I get the shivers just listening to it.

Royal and Caroline came up from the village late this evening. We could see their car lights shining on the trees above the hilltop long before they came in sight — advancing and receding and advancing again as they bucked against the snow drifts in the road. The drifts were deep enough so that Royal had to get out and shovel several times before he could make Popl' Tree Hill. They came in for a few minutes to get warm before they went the rest of the way home. It is comforting to have nice neighbors dropping in on a savage, lonely night like this.

MARCH

TUESDAY, *March 1. Cloudy and warmer. Occasional snow flurries.* Well, Town Meeting is over for another year. Most of the expected fireworks didn't go off. There were more people voting this year than usual and that is a healthy state of affairs for any town.

The meeting dragged through most of the day. At noon, it was adjourned for an hour for dinner. We went downstairs to the town hall dining room, where the women of the Baptist and Congregational Churches had combined to produce the usual Town Meeting dinner of baked beans, hash, pie and coffee, with trimmings of relishes and jellies. It is more than a dinner, it is an informal get-together, where many of the minor differences of the morning are wiped out.

Nothing was decided about remodeling the town hall kitchen, in spite of the interest shown. But an appropriation for the health nurse went through.

The position of road commissioner is usually one of the most contested jobs as it involves spending much of the town's money. And keeping the winter roads passable for automobiles looms large in a country where deep snow is the rule, rather than the exception. The road commissioner chosen this year is especially good, I think.

Of course the school appropriations and the town poor are problems which cause a lot of debate, but most of the discussion was apparently done informally before Town Meeting, for little was said today.

Thursday, March 3. Cold and windy. The milk tester came last night — the regular man. He has had a new son as well as the mumps since he was here last. He told us about both, especially his son.

Father told a good story today. He is a master story-teller in the real Yankee style, with his slow drawl and pithy silences. It was about his own father, who had a very florid complexion.

His father went to a hotel one day, where the hotel keeper offered him a drink and he refused. A little later he was offered another drink and again he refused. Finally, he was offered a drink for the third time and again he said he didn't drink.

"Don't you *ever* drink?" the hotelkeeper asked.

"No," said Grandfather, "never!"

"Well," the hotelkeeper retorted, "then why don't you pull in your sign?"

Saturday, March 5. Stormy. Snow flurries in morning and sleet at night. Just before noon today a little man about five feet tall came to the door. He was looking for work. Rob invited him into the house and I asked him to stay for dinner, so we could tell more about him. We need another man to help during sugaring.

Mr. Bragh, the little man, has certainly had his share of troubles this winter. His wife is in the Brattleboro hospital following a serious operation; he has a daughter and a son in the Bellows Falls hospital, one recovering from pneumonia and the other from intestinal grippe; another child was in the hospital earlier in the winter. He has seven children ranging in age from two-and-a-half to fifteen years. He has had no steady work this winter although he has had odd jobs from time to time.

Rob knew about him and that he was a good worker so he decided to hire him for a month or six weeks during sugaring. He is so little we wonder just how much work he will be able to do, and he doesn't look as if he has had too much to eat lately. He is Bobby's size and Bobby is twelve years old.

Jean's eleventh birthday comes next Friday and we bought the children a pair of roller skates apiece. We had quite a time getting them home without having them suspect anything. We usually give both children some little gift on each birthday. They like to have us do that so neither one feels left out.

Bobby has been looking at bicycles in the store windows and in catalogs. We haven't hurried about getting him one while he was little because of the steep hills on all sides of us, but he is old enough now to be careful.

Sunday, March 6. Warmer. Snow in morning, clear in afternoon. Our doctor went by this afternoon and we wonder if we have a new neighbor yet. Today was the day that Alice, Henry Caine's wife, expected her baby. All of us in the neighborhood are interested. We are always concerned about our neighbors' joys and sorrows. It's entirely different from mere curiosity. But that is hard for outsiders to understand.

Monday, March 7. Windy. Partly cloudy. Alice Caine had a nine-pound baby girl Saturday night.

Sap would run today in the trees if the wind would stop blowing so hard. It's really warm in sheltered places.

John's young brother, Martin, came back with him last night. They arrived after we were all in bed and Martin slept with John on his cot bed. There couldn't have been an oversupply of room. I had told John to let his brother come when he was able, so it was all right. Martin is Bobby's age and they are great friends. He is a tall, dark-haired boy with fine black eyes — a head taller than Bobby.

The three children had a grand time together all day. In the morning they had fun building a (sort of) house out of the branches of a pine tree that had blown down on the edge of the woods in front of the house. When it was finished they tried to sell it. They said it was worth a million dollars but they would sell it to the highest bidder. No one bid on it.

About eleven o'clock this morning they came back to the house and played King and Queen in costume. Martin was Joseph, Bobby was James and Jean was the Queen.

JOSEPH: "What is your wish, Your Majesty?"

QUEEN: "Bring me my drink."

JOSEPH: "I'll bring it on a tray."

QUEEN: "No, Joseph, you stay here." (She looked at his clothes.) "Who dressed you this morning?"

JOSEPH: "James did."

QUEEN: "He didn't do it well. You ought to have a woman do it." (They were dressed in long, flowing robes.)

(JAMES entered with a tray, bearing a tiny dolls' glass of water and a crumb of muffin.)

JOSEPH: "Gee, he gives it to you in large morsels, don't he?"

QUEEN: "You may both be dismissed." . . .

In the afternoon, the two boys walked to the village to a 4-H meeting. Martin went home tonight with his brother. Bobby hated to see him leave and Martin promised to come again soon.

Wednesday, March 9. When I awoke this morning to a brightly shining day, I thought, "This *feels* like sugar weather," and then I wondered how I could express in words the reason for that feeling.

There is a certain bright spiciness in the air. There are cold,

frosty nights and warm, shining days when the eaves drip and the snow melts and winter begins to break away. The air has a different smell — it may be the scent of the sap rising in the trees, or the smell of the earth being released from its frosty coffin — probably a subtle blend of many odors. But it's good. And one never forgets it. Sometimes it mounts as a fever in people's veins, blood runs faster, thoughts run riot, deeds become bolder.

Thursday, March 10. Cloudy and warmer. Jean's birthday is tomorrow — her eleventh. Since Rob had to go to Brattleboro today for the monthly meeting of the directors of the Milk Plant, we all went with him and celebrated the birthday ahead of time.

We chose candles and decorations for the birthday cake, had ice cream sundaes, did some shopping and then went to the movies. The picture was a good comedy and we enjoyed it a lot.

Friday, March 11. Sunny. The weather looked like a good sugar day today — but it wasn't. There was a strong southeast wind blowing and sap wouldn't run.

No one in the cities would dream how important the weather is to the farmer, unless he had some first-hand knowledge. Slight changes in atmospheric conditions, hardly noticed in the city, make all the difference between success and failure to the farmer.

Sap runs best when the *west* wind blows. Why? I don't know, unless it has something to do with the barometric pressure — which may aid or hinder sap being drawn up from the roots of the trees into the branches. When the holes are bored in the trees and sap spouts inserted, the sap runs out through the holes in the trees instead of traveling on up the trunks into the branches. The sap is caught in buckets, which are held in place by hooks attached to the spouts.

It's actually a surprise to many not acquainted with the maple sugar industry that maple syrup does not flow out of the trees and that it takes from one to two barrels of sap to make one gallon of syrup. Trees cannot be tapped too heavily because it shortens the life of the tree.

On one or two days last week sap ran well in warmer sugar lots. Our lots are higher and cooler than some, so sap won't start much here, and what does start, freezes nearly as fast as it drops from the spouts. But we have to be ready, with our equipment all in shape. The sugar season is apt to develop any day now, and the loss of one good run of sap means the loss of many dollars.

If the weather is right this spring, sugar and syrup should be of excellent quality. The leaves on the trees manufacture starches in the summer which revert to sugar in the roots in winter. The heavy foliage borne by the trees last summer should make the sap sweet and fine this spring. There is little snow in the woods, so there will be no deep drifts to hinder collecting the sap. On the other hand, in case of too warm weather, plenty of snow around the roots of the trees keeps the buds from starting and ruining the sap. The whole proceeding is a gamble from start to finish — a gamble on the weather. And no crop control project on earth can control the weather.

Rob still hadn't found an ash crook of the right size in the woods, so he took some straight logs down to Burbee's mill this afternoon to be sawed into the proper sizes for a wood-shed sled.

We were talking, this evening, about a man who helped us during sugaring several years ago. At first Bobby couldn't remember the man but finally he said,

"Oh, I know who you mean. He was the man who was shiny with dirt, wasn't he?"

Jean said tonight that she had a lovely birthday, with her gifts from all the family, and from her grandparents, and her big birthday cake with the lighted candles. She had a party last year, but she decided that her celebration yesterday would take the place of a party today.

Saturday, March 12. Rob has been down in the village all day, working on his sled. He came home for dinner and rushed right back. The sled was finished about five-thirty and he came home to help with the chores. He plans to borrow his father's truck in the morning to bring the sled home.

John and Bobby washed and stacked buckets all day in the back kitchen, with a fire in the stove there so they could keep warm. We usually wash the buckets each spring *after* sugaring, before they are put away, but last year we did the sugaring all alone, we four, and spring planting came before the eleven hundred buckets were all washed. So a few hundred buckets have to be washed this spring. Last year, Rob gathered the sap all alone and I did most of the boiling. The children did what they could, Jean in the house and Bobby at the barn, although there was a lot they couldn't do. We will never try that again. It's too hard.

Two people came this afternoon to have their hair cut. They have to sit on the kitchen stool while I cut around them. But they always come back, so they can't object to the method if the results are satisfactory.

Rob went to Saxtons River tonight and the children and I went with him. The moonlight was beautiful and the night was warm and spring-like. We looked at kitchen stoves and new electric refrigerators. We looked — and came away. Maybe if we have a good sugar season we can get the stove. An electric refrigerator would cost more for us to run than an ice refrigerator, because we have the ice anyway.

Sunday, March 13. Partly cloudy. Warm west wind. The sun was hidden under the clouds most of the day, but the west wind blew gently and sap ran almost a stream.

John was coming back to help today if it was a good sap day,

45

but he may have thought sap wouldn't run because of the uncertain sun, because he didn't appear.

Anyway, after an early dinner, the four of us got into our pants and fixin's and went to the woods to set buckets. We set 226 this afternoon, and the trees were well scattered through the woods. Most of the buckets are fifteen-quart galvanized pails with small holes near the top on one side for hanging to the spouts.

Rob always bores the holes for the spouts with his 7/16-inch auger. He looks the trees over for the best places to bore; some trees have more branches on one side than on the other and that side yields more sap. Today, he said that sap ran best on the north side of the trees. He thought we would have to make what syrup we made in a hurry. Usually, sap runs best on the south side, where the sun shines warmest. Today was almost too warm.

I tapped in the spouts with a hammer, Bobby hung the buckets under the spouts and Jean put on the covers. It was *fun*. We always like this part of sugaring.

There is quite a knack to driving spouts as well as to boring the holes. Naturally, they must be driven into the tree straight, so that the hanger for the buckets is directly underneath; but more than that, the spouts must be driven in just far enough and no farther. An extra tap with the hammer may split the bark on a thin-bark tree, which damages a tree and causes the sap to run away into the ground. On the other hand, on a tree with thick bark, the spout must be driven deeper to reach the rising flow of sap. It is interesting work and the woods are nice this time of year. The sun is getting high enough in the sky to give warmth. There is the odor of sap rising in the trees, earth scents rise from the ground where the snow has melted. There is the feeling of new life in the deeper blueness of the sky, the fleeciness of the clouds, the bracing air.

46

Monday, March 14. Clear. 28 degrees above zero at 8:00 A.M. We set 525 buckets today, a good day's work with the trees so scattered. I was out all day driving spouts. We set 275 buckets this morning and I drove all the spouts but a few, where the trees were up a steep bank slippery with ice. The day was beautiful and quite warm, although it grew colder toward night.

Ruth went out with us this afternoon and helped drive spouts. She enjoyed it as much as the rest of us.

Little Mr. Bragh came this morning to help. He said his people were out of the hospital.

Tuesday, March 15. Ten above zero in the morning. Clear and cold. We now have 1275 buckets set and about 425 more to set. Another good day ought to finish them.

The buckets that were set Sunday have from two to eight quarts of sap in them. We will have to start gathering it soon. Some people in the valleys boiled today for the first time. Rob thinks we will get a storm before sugaring really starts.

We have already received several orders for our first run of new syrup.

The children had to rehearse tonight for their amateur show Thursday evening. Rob was so busy he hated to take them down, so I drove them down in the car. The roads are awfully bumpy, although they are not slippery.

Jean's kitty, Tarzan, who is part of her act, took all the excitement in his stride. She took him to the rehearsal in her arms. They rehearsed in the school house and Bobby put his jacket on one of the desks. Tarzan curled up on the jacket and went to sleep until time for his performance. Jean dressed him in a baby's dress and bonnet, then, cuddling him in her arms like a real baby, she fed him milk from a baby's bottle, nipple and all, while she sang a lullaby. Tarzan is a black kitty with a white bib under his chin and white mitts at the end of black legs. His four little paws curled about the bottle like small hands and his long black tail with a white tip looked funny sticking out below the baby dress. He sucked the nipple with great gusto, oblivious of the laughing audience. After his act he was undressed and went right back to sleep on Bobby's jacket.

Royal brought over some new syrup tonight to test it by our hydrometer. He thought his thermometer was wrong and he wanted to find out for sure. The syrup was nice. A hydrometer is the most accurate way to test the density of syrup, we believe. We always use one for both hot and cold syrup.

Friday, March 18. Cloudy and warmer. The men practically finished setting out the buckets today. Sap started from the trees but didn't run much.

The Parent-Teachers Association held the amateur show last night. Bobby and Ruthy received second prize for their duet, "Sparking Peggy Jane." Jean and Tarzan received honorable mention. The Association cleared over thirty dollars to use toward fixing the school playground.

There was a dance after the show, so we stayed until the children got sleepy. I love to dance and we don't go half often enough. I like the old-fashioned square dances, too, with their grace and swing. Nearly every alternate dance is a square one in our town and in towns around us.

This afternoon we went to Brattleboro, and the Martins went with us. Coming home along the river, the sunset was glorious — flame and saffron and violet and all the shades between. Thelma said it looked as if the gates of Heaven were open and anyone could walk right in. . . .

Saturday, March 19. Roads in Vermont are rough in March. The mud was so deep today that it came up to the running board. When Rob drove back from Saxtons River he thought he'd keep track of the time it took him. As he came into the house he looked at his watch to check up and found that the minute hand had jolted off!

Monday, March 21. Warm and sunny. A beautiful day. This is the first day of spring, warm and lovely. Nearly everyone will be pleased and happy at the warmth — except those who make maple sugar.

We love it — with reservations. It wouldn't take many days like this to start the buds on the trees and spoil sugaring.

Rob and the men gathered all the sap in the woods today, although there wasn't much in each bucket. He started boiling it at six o'clock this afternoon. He intended to start earlier but one of the cows broke away from the barnyard where the cattle were turned out this afternoon, and went up into the pasture. Rob went after her and found her with a new-born calf. He carried the calf home in a bransack slung over his shoulder.

Rob finished boiling at ten o'clock tonight. Every hour that sap stands make the maple syrup a little bit darker, so he likes to boil it in as fast as it comes from the woods. We have made about fifty-two gallons of syrup and there are six or seven gallons left in the evaporator. The heat from the arch, under the evaporator, lasts a long while after the fire is out and plenty of sap has to be left in the evaporator to keep it from burning.

Tuesday, March 22. Fair and warmer. Rob said that since he has been around in the woods, setting buckets, he has seen a number of fine ash trees for sled crooks. But he is all through needing them now. He will have to mark the places so he can remember where they are when he needs them again.

We were astonished to see Alice Caine come walking in with her two-weeks old baby and the girl who is helping her. It is nearly two miles from where she lives to our house, over the worst kind of muddy back-roads, up hills and down. And that little, two-weeks baby was bumped over those roads in a small-wheeled baby carriage. Alice said the baby was colicky!

Rob decided to take what syrup we have to Connecticut, for our customers there, and he wants to start early tomorrow morning. He had to deliver some syrup in Bellows Falls and get some glass bottles for syrup before he could go, and he did that late this afternoon. After he got back I labeled the syrup and got it ready to take, as he filled the containers.

It was after nine o'clock when we finished, and then Rob had to have his hair cut.

I wish I could go with him but one of us has to stay and look after things. Rob suggested that I go in his place and sell the syrup, but he is much better at that than I am. For Connecticut customers, his dry Vermont twang is the best possible proof that they are getting a genuine Vermont product.

Wednesday, March 23. Still too warm. Rob started for Connecticut at seven-thirty this morning. It was such a beautiful day I wanted awfully to go along. Duty, duty!

The men gathered about ten barrels of sap in the north woods and we boiled it into syrup this afternoon. I boiled alone until the men got back with the last load of sap. It is no small job keeping the fire humping under a fast-boiling, fourteen-foot evaporator and at the same time tending to the sap and syrup at the other end. Many farmers have two men for the job, one for firing and one for boiling.

Maple syrup is usually a $200,000 crop in Windham County alone. Some people estimate that about ten per cent of an average crop has been made. That is high for us. The farmers will be hard hit if this weather keeps up. The retail price of syrup has gone up five per cent already in anticipation of a short season.

Thursday, March 24. Last night I awoke from a sound sleep, hearing a downstairs door open and shut, and then steps on the stairs. I turned on the light quickly, alarmed, and called out. It was only Rob, grinning at me. I didn't expect him home until tomorrow, but he had sold all his syrup early and was anxious to get back. I hadn't heard the car drive into the yard and Sammy-dog hadn't barked because he knew his master.

Most of the birds are back and the pussy willows are in

bloom. I love to wake up mornings, hearing the birds sing. It seems almost wicked to want this beautiful, warm, balmy weather to break.

I went into the garden yesterday and dug some parsnips and horseradish roots. I dug only a little horseradish because the ground was frozen three inches below the surface in the horseradish patch, and the roots kept breaking off. It is always a wonder to me, the way horseradish will continue to grow and spread year after year if only the tops are stuck back in the ground.

Friday, March 25. Clear and cooler. The thermometer registered twenty-eight degrees last night. We doubted if the ground froze enough to make the sap run — but it did! It is running almost a stream. Some buckets are full and some are running over.

The men had to stop and fix the sap sled. There is no snow in the woods, and even the wood-shod sled drew awfully hard over the mud when the sap tub was full (it holds seven barrels of sap). So the men rigged a set of two small iron wheels for the front and made a long wooden dray to hold the sap tub.

They gathered sap until after seven o'clock tonight, when it was so dark they were unable to see what they were doing. There is still a lot more in the woods; Rob estimates there are over a hundred barrels still out.

The weather report for tomorrow predicts showers. Never mind, the buckets are covered. Tomorrow will be a busy, hectic day but, glory, we are *glad!* Every one of us will have to work to the limit.

Tonight there was the most brilliant display of northern lights I've ever seen. The lights streaked up the northern sky, receded, and flared again into varying patterns and shapes. The maple tree at the corner of the house was silhouetted against the brightness, its bare, symmetrical branches standing out like an etching. When the northern lights flame, it is said to be a sign of colder weather coming.

Saturday, March 26. Cloudy in morning, snow in afternoon. This is one of those days when nearly everything happens, and you wish some of it hadn't.

Rob got up at 4:00 A.M. and started boiling sap as soon as some of the chores were done. I went out to the sugar house and boiled while Rob caught up on some of his work, ate his breakfast and loaded the milk cans into the car. Then I took the milk to the main road where the milk truck picks it up.

Sap boiled away fast this morning, but at noon, when I went out to relieve Rob so he could eat his dinner, it had slowed down until it merely simmered, in spite of a hot fire in the arch. Snow began to fall heavy and fast, the flakes big and feathery. Sugar snow, it is called.

Going down to the village for Miss Darby whom we had invited up for this afternoon, snow caked on the car windshield so thickly the windshield wiper wouldn't work. I had to get out every few rods to wipe it clear so I could see the road. Finally, I turned down the car window and stuck my head out and drove that way. The roads were terrible — rough and slippery.

Anyway, we had a good time after we got here and Miss Darby apparently enjoyed herself. We had sugar on snow for her. There was plenty of nice new snow for all we wanted. It tastes like nothing else — sticky and icy cold from snow crystals on the outside, hot and still almost liquid on the inside.

Sunday, March 27. Clear and cold. Mr. Bragh and John went to Brattleboro last night, and this morning Mr. Bragh was well soaked — inside. He made many trips to his room after reinforcements, during the morning. He *did* manage to drive the horses well enough to gather a few barrels of sap, but we held our breaths while he was gone for fear he would get the horses tangled up in the woods.

Ruth's young man and her two brothers came toward evening and had sugar-on-snow with us, with the customary trimmings of pickles and doughnuts. It sounds like a queer combination, but it is just right and it surely hits the spot!

Monday, March 28. Slightly warmer. Sunny. Rob sold all the dark syrup today to a commission house that was clamoring for syrup without being able to get any. We don't sell any of our good syrup that way.

John said he was measured for height when he was home last night. He is six feet two in his stocking feet and he hopes he won't keep growing. He is slender but well-built, with broad straight shoulders, and his posture is good. He has a nice smile and a fine, broad forehead. If only I could suggest giving him a good haircut. His hair jumps off suddenly, half-way down his head, as though it had been cut with the aid of a bowl. His appearance is quite a contrast to that of Mr. Bragh.

Mr. Bragh cannot be an inch over five feet tall, and he looks like a little boy from behind, until he starts walking. His step is heavy and plodding like an old man's. There is something about his face that I don't care for, a certain shiftiness to his eyes, with their loose, drooping lids. His chin is weak and his mouth sensuous. He is a capable man, but he is his own worst enemy, and tries to get out of work when the boss isn't looking.

Wednesday, March 30. Cloudy, with light rain beginning at noon. I have boiled for four or five hours each day, but haven't fired much. The big, four-foot logs are pretty heavy to lift after the first hour of it, firing every five minutes and tending to the syrup the rest of the time. It keeps one person on the run all the time. So one of the men has stayed around to fire. We have made only 175 gallons of syrup so far. We should make 400 gallons if the season holds good.

The white maple trees on our front lawn are already red with buds. But they always bloom before the rock maple trees, which are the ones tapped for sap. There is no snow left from the storm last Saturday to keep the roots cool, and the black mud draws the heat terribly.

In spite of all our care with the sap, gathering it in quickly and boiling it at once, the heat has made it darken and the finished product is only Grade A and Grade B. Hardly any of it is Fancy.

The doctor stopped this afternoon and watched us boil down the sap after he returned from calling on the baby that had been born to Royal and Caroline yesterday.

APRIL

FRIDAY, *April 1. Windy, cool and fair.* I raked a corner of the lawn next to the south side of the house this morning so the Golden Glows can grow. Out in the garden I saw the bluest bluebird sitting on a last year's cornstalk. He watched me for a minute and then flew away, his sapphire wings and crimson breast a brave splash of color against the gray of early spring.

I looked for some new rhubarb and found some small, red-tipped heads poking up through the soft, moist earth. I'm hungry for all the fresh spring things to eat, especially rhubarb and dandelion greens.

The children have had a thrilling time all day April Fooling everybody. They pretended to see deer in the mowings (we often do), they put salt in the sugar, pepper on the bread, and all sorts of crazy stunts. It has been fun but rather wearing.

Sunday, April 3. Clear, cold, light frost last night. Rob started to "rim out" the spout holes in the maple trees this morning because many of the holes had dried up and the sap wouldn't run. His rimmer didn't work well, however, so he bored new holes in the trees.

I tried to have him rest today. He is tired and has a cold, but he says he must work in order to make more syrup. He said, "If the Lord doesn't want us to work on Sunday, why does He always send the best sugar weather on Sundays?" And what answer could I give to *that?* He has an answer ready for everything, and usually it is good logic.

Jed Hill came in the late afternoon and had his hair cut. He stayed to supper and during the early part of the evening. He likes to be here Sunday nights although he sometimes fares lightly for supper. Our family prefers crackers and milk for the main course Sunday nights and that, with the dessert, is about all we usually have. But Jed cannot drink raw milk, he says. He can eat butter or cream from the same milk, but never the plain milk!

Tuesday, April 5. Cold, partly cloudy. The flavor of the syrup we are making now is not quite so good as that made during the first of the season. It has a very slight, barely distinguishable buddy taste. Rob has noticed that the sap in the storage tank has a light silvery sheen this morning, which usually means that the buds on the trees are beginning to start.

Wednesday, April 6. Cold, partly cloudy. The Athens overseer of the poor came over here today to see about Mr. Bragh and his family. He surely is in a lot of trouble. "It's an awful mess," he told Rob, and it's all of that. He has a court order to turn over all his money to his wife, but we knew nothing of it until today, so we have paid him as he earned it.

The reports are that his wife is a veritable hell-cat and taunts him by telling him that some of his seven children are not his. But he is supposed to be responsible for supporting them all.

She makes life miserable for him and he gets drunk to forget. And then she gets after him again, and so it goes.

The overseer took him back to Athens this noon to "work up" some wood for his family. The children have been boarded for eight weeks; now the authorities are anxious to collect the family again and have them go back to their home.

Rob received a letter tonight from the man in Connecticut who buys our syrup in large lots. He wants forty or fifty gallons of syrup at once. So Rob plans to take it to Connecticut in the morning, and I plan to go too.

We have been getting the syrup ready this evening. Now it is all labeled.

Rob took the car down to the brook and washed it after dark tonight. There was plenty of water there. He loaded the syrup before we went to bed tonight and we are all ready to start in the morning. Rob's birthday is tomorrow.

Thursday, April 7. Cold, partly cloudy. This has been such a delightful day — and a long one. The alarm clock went off at three but we didn't want to get up at all. We dozed again for half an hour and then snapped into action. By the time the fires were fixed and we were dressed and had our breakfast, it was nearly four-thirty.

As we drove out of the yard, only a thin light line at the horizon cut the edge of darkness in the eastern sky. The world, our part of it, was black with the density which precedes the dawn.

The headlights of our car picked out and reflected the glass window panes of the houses we passed, glimmered on the tin sap buckets hanging on maple trees by the roadside. And the eyes of prowling animals flamed into fire as they hunted near the road.

As we sped into Newfane, eight miles from home, the world was graying in the approaching dawn, and in Brattleboro, eighteen miles away, the street lights and the all-night lights burning in store windows looked incongruous in the full brightness of early morning. Between Greenfield and Northampton the sunrise tinted the fluffy clouds with beautiful pastel colors.

Below Northampton the sky was leaden and overcast. Light snow, new fallen, showed through last year's stubble and brush and the roads were wet and slippery. The farther south we went the more snow we found, and when we reached Litchfield, Connecticut, at eight-thirty in the morning, the ground was covered with three or four inches of snow. Some of the roads had been sanded, and snow plows were out, busily clearing the roads.

We got back to Townshend village a little after five. Three hundred miles is a fair day's jaunt when three or four hours in the middle of the day are consumed in business and pleasure.

I gave Rob his birthday gifts — clothes for use and cigarettes for pleasure — before we left home this morning, while the children were still asleep. But this evening as he came through the door, the children lined up and sang, "Happy Birthday to You."

They came up to me as I was resting, with a look of expectant hopefulness in their eyes. "Is Daddy very tired tonight?" they wanted to know. I knew why they asked, and I told them that he was really dreadfully tired but I thought he wouldn't object to a little fun. So they connived, with Ruth in on the plans, to give him a birthday spanking. After the chores were done they were ready for him with paddles, jump ropes and a fire shovel. They had a hilarious time and Rob kept them excited by returning spanks, occasionally. Ruth made a beautiful birthday cake in three large, graduated layers, topped with white icing and pink candles. The large candles on the table were blown out so we could get the full effect of the candles on the cake.

Friday, April 8. Cloudy. Hard snow storm in afternoon. About four inches. Mr. Haynes, the minister who has been filling in until a new one comes, died suddenly today of a heart attack. All of us feel that we have lost a good friend. He was the kindest man, and he knew how to express his good will. Each person who came in contact with him while he was here felt warmed and a little happier. It's a wonderful quality and it could have come to its full beauty only through constant use.

Sunday, April 10. Fair, cool, strong east wind. Nipper, one of the Percherons, was lame yesterday and worse this morning, so Rob called the veterinarian, Dr. Hopkins. He came this afternoon with his wife, Helen, and their two oldest children, all good friends of ours.

Dr. Hopkins found a triangular shaped pine chip in the frog of Nipper's foot. He dug it out and administered a dose of tetanus antitoxin to prevent lockjaw. The horse seems much better tonight.

Tuesday, April 12. Warm, partly cloudy. Scattered showers in afternoon. I boiled sap today during the noon hour and then hurried to get ready to go to a Health Council meeting in Newfane.

As soon as I got home I changed my clothes, put on my blue denim pants and went out to the sugar house again so Rob would be free to do the chores. The men gathered sap until after dark. Nipper is better but not well enough to travel in the woods and they used old Punch to fill in. Punch is an old Percheron, about twenty-six years old.

The weather turned warm today and the evaporator arch was like a furnace. My pants got so hot that they burned my legs when they brushed against me. Sweat poured from me and my shirt was soon soaked. My legs felt parboiled. Steam rose thickly from the pans of sap and swirled and eddied unceasingly. The cracking of the fire, the soft swishing sound of boiling sap, and the foggy vapor rising from the pans soon made me feel as if I were in a dreamy world of my own. I could barely make out the walls of the sugar house. Watching the sap

59

boil made me think of watching the undulating waves of the ocean for a long period of time, and I began to feel a dangerous lulling of the senses. I knew that one minute of inattention would make the sap burn and would spoil several gallons of syrup so I fought against the drowsiness and strained my eyes through the gloom to bring the syrup to the proper temperature and density.

For the second night we had to work late. It was a beautiful spring night, soft and warm, and the full moon was gorgeous and looked for a while as if it were hung on top of the high smoke stack. Often during the evening I stepped out of the sugar house to watch it. Long trailing clouds of sooty black smoke poured from the smoke stack and rushed across the moon like trailing streamers.

Wednesday, April 13. Warm, cloudy. Our sugar wood gave out today. The season has been so long and strung out that it has taken more wood than usual. The men finished gathering the sap in the woods this morning and Rob boiled in the sap while John cut more wood.

Mr. Bragh's wife sent word that she was ill and wanted him to come home — just as we were the busiest. So I took him over to Athens and Cambridgeport where he tried to find someone to help his wife. He was unsuccessful, so he had to stay with her himself. He said he would try to get a neighbor to stay with his wife tomorrow so he could come back and help gather sap, but somehow, I don't believe he will. We need him badly now, and I hope he can make it.

I stopped at the Overseer's house in Athens and told him that if he expected Mr. Bragh to support his family, he would have to be given a chance to work without being constantly called home.

Everyone went away this evening but the children and me and after the children were in bed I did the machine sewing on my black silk crepe dress. It was all cut out before. It fits well

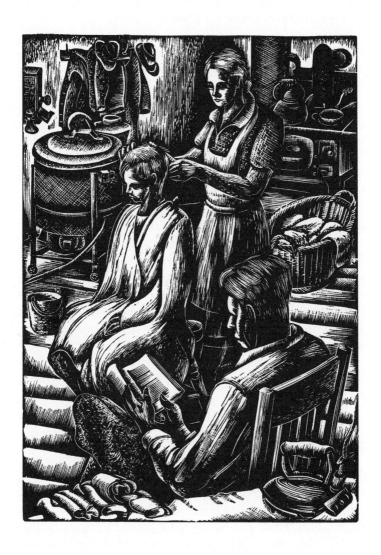

and looks nice with my black coat. I wonder if I will manage to get them finished in time for Easter.

Bobby is working on an essay for a contest sponsored by the Windham County Historical Society. He is writing about the people who have lived in our house during the past 138 years.

When the house was used as a tavern, one Follett ancestor lived here for a time. But it was the children's great-great-grandmother who started the zealous devotion to the place. When she was a girl, living in Athens, the town adjoining Townshend, she could see the farm from the top of the hill on her father's farm. She used to look across the valley between and hope that someday she could live here.

She grew up, married and went to live in Jamaica, Vermont. It was not until after her husband's death, when she was left with two small boys, that her dream was fulfilled and she bought the farm. At that time it consisted of only a hundred acres. She paid for that and added four hundred and fifty more acres. Her sons grew to manhood and went to the Civil War. The younger one was killed in action. The older son, James, returned to live on the farm and became a famous stone bridge builder of his day.

His six children were all born in the big house. After his death, his oldest son, Orison, bought out the others' interests in the old homestead. Orison's three sons were born here. His oldest son, Robert, bought the place from his father after he finished college, about sixteen years ago. No wonder our children feel its ties.

Thursday, April 14. Very warm for this season of the year. Sunny and beautiful. Ruth was called home tonight because her youngest sister was ill. Molly just had her thirteenth birthday and is in Bobby's class in school. She was taken to the hospital this afternoon with a terrific pain in her abdomen.

Friday, April 15. Warm, partly cloudy. Hard rain in afternoon. During the middle of last night I woke up, hearing a car drive into the dooryard. Someone yoo-hooed for Rob. It was his father, wanting him to go with him to Fred Lee's house, about two miles away on a back road. One of Fred's cows was having difficulty calving. Father had worked on her for a hour before he came after Rob. When they got back the poor cow was dead, so their midnight trip was for nothing.

On their way back they got stuck in the mud and it was half past three in the morning before they got home.

At half past six this morning our telephone rang. It was Ruth, crying so hard she could barely talk. Molly had an operation last night. There wasn't much hope except that she was young and strong. Ruth promised to keep me informed but it looked as if she would be unable to come back to work for a while.

At eight in the morning a neighbor telephoned in place of Ruth. Molly was dead.

The children — all the children in town — and the parents, too, are badly shaken. This second tragedy has struck so soon after the other, that every one wonders what will come next.

Bobby says over and over, "I thought nothing serious ever happened to school children."

Saturday, April 16. Beautiful day, sunny and warm. Jed Hill came to have his hair cut today, but I did manage, between jobs, to make the bound buttonholes on my coat and finish my dress. So I'm all set for the Easter Parade! I fixed over my black hat with the white doo-dad on it and made over one of my gray-blue hats into a cute little bonnet with blue ribbons on it for Jean. She has a nice blue coat and a red taffeta dress with blue ribbons at the neck and waist that she got for Christmas. So she is all fixed too.

Bobby wondered what *he* could wear for Easter. I persuaded him that his best suit was fine, long pants and all.

Sunday, April 17. Easter Sunday. Colder — Partly cloudy in the afternoon but beautifully bright in the morning.

We went to church this morning, all of us, but Rob was late because he wanted to see Puffer about trucking the sugaring apparatus he bought in Connecticut. Puffer will do it for ten cents a mile, and may want to buy some of the buckets.

Bobby was to sing a solo part in one of the Easter anthems. He sat in the church choir, with his black robe, white collar and all. During the first anthem I saw him sit down suddenly and put his hand to his head. I watched him anxiously and saw that he was pale and acted as if he felt faint.

Finally, I decided that he wasn't getting better and might get worse, so I went up the aisle of the church while the choir leader was helping him to his feet. I helped him down the choir steps at the corner of the pulpit and led him outdoors.

"Gracious," I thought, "What can be the matter? He never did this before." I got some water for him to drink and put some on his head and neck. He had begun to feel better when I heard music coming softly from inside the church. "Listen," I said.

It was Bobby's song he had been so anxious to sing, being sung by the tenor soloist. It sounded beautiful.

"That's a nice song," Bobby said philosophically, as he wiped his damp forehead with his coat sleeve.

We went back into the church after a while when Bobby felt better, but he sat in the pew with me and didn't go back into the choir. I thought the strain and nervous tension of the past few days had been too much for him.

In the afternoon I left the family by themselves and went down to the village to Molly's funeral, which was held in the Baptist Church. It was the saddest funeral I have attended for a long time.

Bobby had some fever when I got home and we called the doctor. He found that Bobby had a touch of grippe; apparently nothing serious but he must stay in bed tomorrow and keep quiet. That was the trouble with him this morning. I would never have let him go if I had known.

Monday, April 18. Cloudy, rain. Regular April showers. Two new calves came at the barn last night. When Rob went up at eleven he saw only one cow about to calve, so he put her in the calving pen. She had a husky bull calf, part Holstein, from Lewis' bull that got into our pasture last summer. Annabelle, a purebred Guernsey, had calved in her stanchion and her beautiful big heifer calf had fallen in the trench, striking against the concrete, and had died. It must have weighed ninety pounds and that is big for a Guernsey calf. We would have liked to raise the heifer but Rob sold the bull calf for veal.

This warm rain has started green things growing rapidly. You can almost see them shooting up. The iris have grown a full two inches today. The white maples are in bloom and their red flowers are gorgeous. When I look off over the fields toward the woods I can see occasional flame-tipped trees which I know are the white maples; they are the only trees around which look just like that.

Nearly every day I go down into the old barnyard where the barn used to be years ago and look at the rhubarb Rob's great-grandmother must have planted there — lovely red rhubarb. Today the biggest leaves measured a full three inches across and the ruby stalks were an inch long. I can hardly wait.

Wednesday, April 20. Warm and sunny. Bobby arose bright and early this morning and said he felt fine; he was going to school. He wasn't going to miss seeing "Snow White" in Brattleboro tomorrow.

Not to be fooled by appearances I took his temperature. It was 100.3. So again Bobby went back to bed, much to his disgust, even dismay. He has learned to take his temperature himself and has taken it about every hour all day. He has been very docile and quiet and he is determined to get his fever down as quickly as possible. When he took his temperature at noon it was down to normal and has been ever since. He really feels quite well today.

He worked for a long while on his spelling words, writing those he missed ten times apiece until he was sure of them. Then I gave him the words to write. He got them all right. This new interest in spelling is having its effect on his other subjects. Spelling was one of his weakest subjects. Now he has learned that he can get any mark he wants to, if he works for it, and he is applying that knowledge to his other studies. Previously he had been interested mostly in passing marks and saw no reason to exert himself further.

Thursday, April 21. Cooler. Partly cloudy. All the schools in town had solid sessions this morning. The Parent-Teachers Association chartered Osborne's bus to take the graded school children to Brattleboro to see "Snow White." Mr. Pinkham drove his bus down with some graded school children as well as some high school students. I heard there were seventy-two youngsters who went, but I think there were more.

The movie was good and the children thought it was perfect, but I was vaguely disappointed in places, mostly because of the jerky unreality of Snow White, the Prince, and the Queen. Of course the birds and beasts and dwarfs were unreal too, but they appeared more logical in the fairy story than (supposedly) human characters. I heard afterward that Walt Disney was not satisfied with those characters, but that humans move so much more slowly than animals that it was difficult to animate them properly. The children were entranced. They loved every scene.

Saturday, April 23. Bright and sunny. Brisk wind. I heard a bear hooting in the woods last night. We almost never see them around here but we sometimes hear them as they go through the woods. The children saw one several years ago. They were too little to realize what it was but from their description we were sure it was a bear. We kept them close to the house for a while after that for Rob saw traces of where they had been, but nothing more. There have been numerous bear shot in nearby towns.

Sunday, April 24. Sunny and cool. Jean and Bobby went into the woods today and gathered long branches of white, fairy-like shad blossoms. I put them in two tall vases and set them on the serving table in the dining room, one at each end. They look like prints of Japanese cherry blossoms. They were mostly in bud when the children brought them in but they are opening in the warmth of the room. Shad blossoms are beautiful to look at but rather disappointing to smell, and they fade quickly in the house.

The children stayed outdoors in the bright sunshine nearly all day. The ground is still so wet that they cannot sit down on it.

The line of white birch trees which grow by the pasture wall is a maze of beautiful, new, delicate green leaves. White birches always are among the first trees to get their leaves each spring, and they are such a lovely color — a bright, tender green, exquisite against the stark whiteness of their trunks and branches.

We changed our clocks last night. We moved them ahead an hour as we plan to go on daylight saving time for the summer. We had to do it in self-defense. School is going on the new time and so does the milk. It must be down to the main road by six-fifteen standard time. I doubt if we go to bed any earlier. We had to get up before dawn to get the milk ready in time.

We don't like daylight saving time much here, where we have to work by the sun and the drying off of the dew, which things don't change at all, whatever way we manipulate our clocks.

Monday, April 25. Cloudy, windy and cool. Occasional bursts of sunshine. This is real April weather. Yesterday, only the birch trees showed a froth of green leaves, today the poplar, elm and willow trees are bright with varying shades of green; no two alike. The white maples are still decked out in red blossoms. On close inspection, other species of trees show tiny leaves just breaking out of their buds.

Friday, April 29. Rob went to Connecticut again yesterday with maple sugar and syrup. His father went with him. They got back at five o'clock tonight.

There were a number of thundershowers late last night and today. They are still going on. The radio snaps and crackles. It has a lightning arrester, and I hope it works.

The out-of-doors grows more glorious each day. There are now more shades of green in the meadows and woods than one would imagine there could be. The small, new leaves on the white maple trees look like dainty parachutes above the trailing red flowerets; the rock maple flowers resemble long, green fringe strung all over the trees. The grass on the lawn is nearly high enough to be cut. The shad are blossomed full and the plum trees are budded.

We have had rhubarb sauce, and the dandelion greens are large enough to eat. I planned to pick enough for a meal tonight, but everything outdoors is drenched with rain.

The milk tester came tonight.

Saturday, April 30. Cloudy and cool. The milk tester had to do his testing in the kitchen, as usual. As he needs the kitchen table, the sink and stove, I have to plan my work in the limited space he leaves. It's not an easy task any morning, but it is especially hard on a Saturday morning.

This also was the day when the men in town helped fix the new playground back of the school house and the women got dinner at the school house for the men who worked. The four-room school house has three teachers. The fourth room houses the town library.

Rob and John went down to help about ten o'clock this morning. I went with them, intending to help the women with the dinner for a while and then go home to get dinner for the children and the milk tester. But I had sort of a hunch that I might be away longer than I expected, so I planned a dinner the children could get if necessary, and Jean started to make a cake before I left. It was well that I did.

The teacher of the three upper grades was all alone at the school house when I got there, except for some of the school girls. She had her head in her hands trying to think what to do about dinner. She wasn't used to anything like this. Several women in town were cooking big dishes of scalloped macaroni but the school director thought the men needed something more hearty for food when they were shoveling gravel, something like beef stew. The teacher didn't know how to make it, so I lent a hand.

Beef stew was ready at twelve-fifteen, when the men came in. Other townspeople sent or brought pies and doughnuts and pickles and we made coffee. More women came at noon and helped serve the dinner and wash the dishes afterward.

The men drew about a hundred loads of gravel onto the playground. That was a good start, but it still needs nearly two more days' work. Three trucks worked all day. The services of all the helpers were donated free of charge. I believe the gas was furnished by the Parent-Teachers Association.

The Lohmons came tonight to Deerbrook Camp. They stopped here to get enough water to last until they get theirs started. It was good to see them again.

MAY

S UNDAY, *May 1. Sunny and bright. Fairly warm this morning.* This was the first day of fishing season, and Rob and Bobby went fishing this morning. Rob caught eight trout and Bobby caught two. We had them for dinner, fried in egg and cornmeal, and they were delicious. Rob said the brooks were lined so thick with fishermen he wondered how anyone could catch anything.

Monday, May 2. Sunny and warm; brisk wind blowing. My washing was out early this morning, and I was hanging the last few pieces on the line when Anna Eddy came to spend the day. We had a delightful time together.

After dinner, we walked over the hills. The woods are almost unbelievably splendid in their pale colorings, with the very blue sky overhead and the soft fleecy white clouds making changing patterns of light and shadow on the mountains and valleys.

We found an old cellar hole where some family long ago had worked to build a home. Now, nothing is standing but a few

70

foundation stones. We could trace the positions of the barns and sheds and gates by the stone walls and the grass-grown foundations. There were plum trees in full bloom, standing where some loving hand had planted them. And lilac bushes and apple trees. It made me feel sad to think of the end of all their hopes and planning. Even the road that used to run by their house has long since been abandoned and is now only a lane through a pasture.

Wednesday, May 4. Sunny and warmer but still tangy. Rob ordered fifty pounds of peas today from the Eastern States Farmer's Exchange. We plan to raise them to sell.

The Alma Kidder house in Townshend village burned to the ground this afternoon. Rob went down to help fight the fire, as every able-bodied man in town is expected to do. We might need help ourselves some time. We were making maple sugar when the telephone gave the alarm and someone had to stay with it until it was done, or spoil the whole batch. So I stayed.

After Rob got back from the fire, I took the car and went to Newfane to the last Health Council meeting before the big day next Friday. It ought to be an inspiring meeting and it lasts all day and during the evening. All the towns in the county are cooperating.

A town official told of a little two-year-old boy who had pneumonia. His parents were poor and ignorant and no-account, but the boy needed expert nursing if he were to pull through. The town official went to a nurse who lived in his town and told her:

"I wish you would take the case for the sake of humanity. He *must* be given a chance. You will have to take everything you need with you. They haven't a thing. All the bedroom furnishings consist of a bed, a mattress and a blanket; they keep warm with the stove. And they drink like fish. But they need you, and they need you badly."

The nurse went, and the boy pulled through. For what? We wonder.

Thursday, May 5. Beautiful, sunny and warm. This morning I had to decide among four different jobs that needed doing besides my regular household tasks. The house must be cleaned; there is urgent need for some raking and planting to be done out-doors; I have a lot of sewing which must be done; and I *want* to write a story which I have had in my head for a long time, more than anything else.

I finally cleaned my living room. If cleanliness is really next to godliness, then my choice was all right. I like the century-old tavern except at house cleaning time and then it grows and swells, I swear it does, until it is as big as a medieval castle. And all that light paint to wash! Once I dreamed of wandering through endless rooms in my house, always coming upon a different room I never saw before, and wondering what on earth I could ever do with it!

All but six rooms are cleaned tonight. I am very tired and every time I get comfortably settled on the couch or in a chair, Rob calls me, wanting help. That syrup! Will it ever be finished?

Bobby's teacher sent a note home tonight by Bobby. She said his hygiene notebook was very badly done. I looked at it and it didn't show much enthusiasm. She wrote, "Do you think that you could help impress upon him that his work must be satis-factory or he will have to remain in grade seven next year. He has a good mind and I want to see him in the eighth grade next year."

Now, just *what* shall I tell him? I showed him the note but he called the hygiene notebook "that old thing" and didn't feel it was important enough to bother with, although he studies his other subjects at home. I can vividly remember a hygiene notebook I had to make when I was a child — not by the material which was supposed to go into it but by the distaste I felt in having to do it. Maybe that is the way Bobby feels.

Friday, May 6. Rainy and cool. A light frost fell last night but nothing was damaged here.

The Health Institute was apparently a great success. Everything clicked. There was a large, appreciative audience during the day and evening. School boards in the towns around had their schools keep a solid session during the morning so the teachers could attend the programs in the afternoon and evening.

The century-old Court House on Newfane Common, with its walls hung with oil portraits of sober judges of bygone days, was an interesting setting for the modern medical and social welfare institute. The speakers were mostly of state or national reputation. The governor of Vermont spoke and members of the State Board of Health and the Public Welfare Department. The speech which received the most favorable comment was one which couldn't have been given in public a few years ago: "Some Newer Aspects of Social Hygiene."

The speaker declared that, while there was great need of education to prevent the spread of venereal diseases, the subject should not receive undue emphasis. It should be taught normally, with other aspects of health and social hygiene, and the people afflicted should not be treated as social pariahs. He didn't mince words and his talk was clear and clean. People liked it immensely. Many things the older generation didn't understand he explained and suggested ways of presenting the facts to children.

Afterward, I heard one of the younger women blame the older generation for withholding so many necessary facts, or hedging, when talking to their children. But an older woman spoke up,

"I don't think they can be blamed so much," she said, "They didn't know these things themselves. Nobody told them and there was no way for them to find out. How *could* they tell us?"

I wanted to attend the evening session, but Rob had to go to

73

Springfield and he needed the car. The children and I went with him.

The night was lovely. The full moon rode high as we came home. She wore gauzy skirts flung about her tonight, a sign of more stormy weather, but they lent an added enchantment to the darkened hills and valleys and the slowly rising mists along the brooks.

Saturday, May 7. Cloudy, cool. I cut two heads of hair this morning. Saturday morning is a bad time for a housewife to stop work for an hour, but I managed to work the hair-cuts in all right.

The hat blocks were brought up from the Farm Bureau office yesterday and left at the store and I brought them home from there. I have two days to use the blocks so I blocked a summer felt hat today. It looks as good as new. A brown straw hat is still on the hat blocks, drying. Mother is coming up Monday to block her hats. I still have a black straw and a white straw to renovate. And then won't I be well fixed for hats? Especially as I prefer to go hatless whenever I can.

The children started cleaning their rooms yesterday and finished them this morning, except for the bureau drawers. I helped them put up their new curtains. Bobby's are a sunny yellow with ruffled edges, and Jean's are white trimmed with red windmills and little Dutch children. Both children are very much pleased with their rooms and themselves.

Mother's Day is tomorrow and I have been getting Mother's gift ready. I couldn't find anything nice enough, so I wrote a poem for her to go with the gift.

Rob harrowed with his tractor bush-and-bog harrow after supper tonight, until dark. Quite a large piece of ground is all ready for planting.

The apple blossoms are out in all their fragrance and beauty. Jean filled all our vases but one with sprays of apple blossoms.

That one she filled with wood violets of white and lavender and their green, heart-shaped leaves.

Sunday, May 8. Partly cloudy. Cool. The youngsters told me to sleep as long as I wanted to this morning. It was Mother's Day and they would get breakfast. When I arose at nine, the family was eating breakfast. The children had made pancakes which were a credit to them. They wished me a happy Mother's Day.

Then, after being so angelic, they fell from grace and argued and fought while they were doing the dishes.

The children wanted to make a cake for me for Mother's Day but my birthday is tomorrow and they were unable to decide whether to make a cake today or tomorrow. They finally made it today and will frost and decorate it tomorrow. Chocolate cake is their own favorite, so that is what they decided to make.

After they argued for some time about who would make the cake and who would frost it, Bobby made it. He had never made a cake before and he wondered what the recipe meant when it said, "cream the shortening." With all the supervision necessary, I could have made several cakes during the time it took, but they wouldn't have tasted half so good.

Monday, May 9. Sunny and bright. Windy. The children stood beside their chairs at the breakfast table this morning and sang, "Happy Birthday to You."

They had a hard time deciding when to decorate the cake, but they waited until they got home from school this afternoon. They took some of their own money to buy a blue candy alphabet so they could write "Happy Birthday, Mother" on the cake. After they started to put it on, they realized there were no two letters alike in the candy alphabet, and that the words "Happy Birthday, Mother" require several alike. They were terribly disappointed at first, but decided to make the best of it and put on the letters they had.

They brought the cake to the table, resplendent with *ten* candles and an inscription that read: "Hapy Bird, Mogun," and an *x* marked the lowest spot on the cake. It was light and delicious, and I never ate one that tasted better.

Tuesday, May 10. All kinds of weather: a little sun, a little rain, some thunder and lightning. I went to Brattleboro with Rob when he went to his Milk Plant meeting. We started about eleven. I fixed dinner for John before we went. He is plowing the lot above the barn for potatoes.

We went over Putney Mountain to Governor Aiken's nursery in Putney. Rob wanted to see about getting the raspberry and strawberry plants which were ordered last fall. The drive over the mountain was beautiful, and the roads, although rough, were in better shape than we expected. The mud holes had dried out considerably.

Wednesday, May 11. Cloudy in morning, clear and cooler in afternoon. The weather report predicts light frosts tonight in exposed places.

Rob has been getting the ground ready for the strawberry plants. My brother Everett came this afternoon to help him. They set out over four hundred plants.

John plowed the west lot today, where the oats are to be planted and Rob harrowed it with his tractor after supper. It is time for the oats to be planted.

Thursday, May 12. Cold and cloudy. Rob went to Putney early this morning after the berry plants. He and Everett finished setting out the strawberries.

The lilacs are budded in long purple spikes. But the weather is so cold and damp we have to keep the doors closed and the wood fire going in the kitchen stove. We lit the fire in the living-room fireplace this afternoon, and it felt good.

There was a light frost last night along the brooks but it

apparently did no damage in this section. There was a heavy frost in Putney which must have damaged the apple orchards considerably.

I finished cleaning the downstairs rooms today except for a few more windows to wash. In the afternoon I made cake and brownies and cooked sugar syrup for punch.

John and Marion Hooper of Stephen Daye Press and their friends the Baldwins stopped in this evening — Arthur Baldwin writes sea stories for boys. I greatly enjoyed meeting them and talking with them and the Hoopers. John Hooper suggested that I leave the novel I was writing and keep a journal of our everyday life here on the farm. I was disappointed, but pleased that I'd kept up the diary I started last fall. John persuaded me to believe that people would be more interested in what a farmer's life is honestly like, than in any story I might make up. I hope he's right!

Even though I enjoy doing many things, I would like most of all to have more time to write. But somehow I have a hunch that in order to do any job well, my close human relationships must first be right, and that if I neglect my children and my family at this stage of the game, we would all be poorer in the long run. Maybe I am wrong. Maybe they would be just as well off without me. But I cannot make myself believe that. I have tried it for short intervals and it has never worked out well. The youngsters need someone to whom they may go at any time, anywhere, to discuss their problems. Sometimes, I am not much help and I make mistakes, but I try, and I listen.

Friday, May 13. Cold, cloudy. Occasional showers. Rob and Everett set out the last of the raspberry plants today. John has been plowing steadily for the past few days. Rob said he has done a fine job, but John, like a true craftsman, said he wished it was better. He takes a real interest in his work here. He is a nice boy and pleasant to have around.

The Home Demonstration meeting began at 1:00 P.M. at the

Town Hall. The meeting was on Family Finance and I was especially anxious to attend. We had a nice buffet luncheon, with everyone furnishing something. I took cupcakes. Mother and Jean went with me.

After the luncheon a speaker talked on the Federal Housing Bill and bank loans. Then we had a discussion on the different sources of rural income, and the recession of farm folks from farms to villages and cities. We decided that diversified farming in this section of the country is about the only way to balance the budget. I could have added that, even with an income from diversified farming, the present day farmer is a long way from being well off.

Saturday, May 14. Warmer and sunny. Bobby, Jean and I went to the meeting of the Southern Music Educator's Club in the afternoon. Groups of school children from several surrounding towns sang and danced. In the number given by the Townshend Graded School, Bobby was soloist and was supported by a chorus of children singing alto and soprano.

Bobby's music teacher came to me before the program and said,

"I think you are going to be very proud of your son Robert's singing today. He has a beautiful voice."

Sunday, May 15. Hard rain. Cold. Rob worked on his farm accounts today and I wrote a few letters and read by the open fire. The children have been uneasy, starting to do many things without much interest. Rainy days are hard on children, especially when they have to be cooped up inside a house. But for grown-ups who have worked hard during the week, a rainy day is a blessing. It relaxes us and makes us want to rest our bodies. And when we have an open fire to sit beside, it is sweet content.

Monday, May 16. Very cold, cloudy and windy. A foot of snow fell in Stratton Mountain yesterday and an inch fell in Windham.

Stratton looks like one of the Alps this morning. Leaves and flowers do not look injured around this section, but if the clouds clear away so that frost falls, extremely serious damage will be done to the fruit crops in New England. The wind blows in shivery gusts about the house, and the leaves swish lonesomely.

The unease of the wind and the low temperature make me feel uneasy and blue, too. Without meaning to, I stop my work occasionally and wander about the house without direction or purpose. I feel impatient with people and things.

I tried to settle down to sew this morning. It was too cold to wash walls and windows. Rob wanted a warmer pair of trousers, and they needed mending before they could be worn. Then we discovered that his barn jumper had a hole between the shoulders where a spark had fallen from the fire in the village. That was fraying out and had to have a patch put on. Then I began fixing my red wool jacket. But I couldn't do it. Finally I gave in to my desire; I wanted to write a story which has been trying to get itself written for some time. How *good* it was to do it.

Tuesday, May 17. Fair and warmer. It is beautiful today with a brisk wind blowing. Birds and frogs sing loudly and happily. The beautiful colorings in the fields and woods have lasted longer than usual this year — and the fruit blossoms, too. The woods are still filled with soft reds, yellows and browns to contrast with the many-colored greens.

My washing dried fast. The clothes looked so white and fresh swinging in the wind.

Bobby said he was dreadfully embarrassed today in school.

"I was never so mad . . . well . . . not mad but disgusted as when it happened. What do you suppose little Jill Brown, a first-grader, did to me? She hugged me right in front of all the rest of the kids. One of the girls asked Jill who she liked the best, and she put her arms right around me. O-h-h, it was *terrible*. I didn't know what to do. I didn't want to hurt her feelings, so I said, 'Why don't you go outdoors and play?' She went, but wasn't that an awful thing to happen? Right in school, too!"

Rob harrowed in an acre and a half of oats with his tractor and harrow after supper. He sowed them this afternoon. He was afraid to leave them until morning because the birds might eat them up.

Thursday, May 19. Partly cloudy. Warmer. Rob finished planting thirty-seven rows of peas today. We hope to have bushels to sell. He also put nitrate of soda around the currant and the blueberry bushes to fertilize them.

John mowed the lawn as long as he could see tonight. He wasn't asked to, he just did it to be nice. Rob's uncle said ours wasn't a lawn, it was an estate. It is large enough to be.

I trimmed rose bushes and other shrubs. They should have been done a month ago.

Saturday, May 21. Cloudy in morning. Clear and warmer in afternoon. Cool wind. Ned Benton called Rob on the telephone this morning to ask about the corrosive sublimate solution used to soak seed potatoes in, to prevent some diseases. Many of the farmers around here ask Rob's advice on farm problems and he helps gladly. His agricultural training in college, as well as his experience before and since, have made him well qualified to answer questions.

The people of the town held a fire prevention meeting tonight, to talk over plans for fire equipment. Rob went to the meeting. They were unable to decide anything definite, although something needs to be done, badly. It will take another bad fire to get real action.

Sunday, May 22. Fair, cool except in the sun. Fred Lee's calves got out again early this morning and came tramping over here. We tried to chase them kindly until they wallowed through our vegetable garden where the plants are just coming up and went on into the strawberry bed. That was just too much and Rob sicked the dog onto them. They lingered no longer but cleared out in a hurry. There is no need of their getting out, only Fred is too lazy to fix his fences.

Monday, May 23. Cloudy in morning, rain in afternoon. Bobby is sending for his tent in the morning. He has been saving his money for some time so he could get it. We added enough to the money he had to make up the balance. His birthday comes on June ninth and we called it a birthday present. He is thrilled to pieces and he plans to sleep in it during the summer.

Tuesday, May 24. Showers. Cooler. I have been thinking today, strangely, of the time a famous author came to our home. It happened several years ago and I haven't thought of it for a long time. She came incognito. . . .

It was this way: we were planning to sell our house and farm at that time and it was in the hands of a real-estate agent. One Sunday in late autumn my mother and father and all our family were sitting around the living room stove as the day closed into dusk. A car drove up to the house, and the real-estate agent stepped out and came to the door. The agent said he had some prospective customers for the place.

A middle-aged woman and a man came into the house with no introductions. I thought that was strange but decided that probably it was an oversight on the part of the agent. During the time I was showing them about the house I kept wondering about them. She was kindly and interested and warmly human. She looked as if she had recently spent hours in a beauty parlor. Her rather full face looked well cared for, her skin had that pink-and-whiteness obtained only by assiduous care. Her black, turbaned hat had a becoming band of white next to her face.

I assumed that her companion was her husband and yet there was something. . . . He was just the opposite in appearance from her. He was big and tall and rugged. His face was lined and creased by the weather. His hair was rough and badly combed. While she looked like a product of the cities, he was manifestly an outdoor man. One could imagine him a farmer. I wondered at their attraction for each other unless it was the attraction of opposites.

"But she isn't so soft as she looks," I said to myself.

They were here probably half an hour in all. But the real-estate agent was so impressed by his customers' names that he was unable to leave without spilling the news. He sneaked away from the rest of us and told Mother, warning her not to tell until they were gone. She was a famous author and he a noted explorer. They didn't come back. I saw a newspaper clipping about them the next day. I wondered if they ever found a house and I wondered . . . many things.

Rob went on to Saxtons River this morning when he took the milk, to get the air washer on his tractor soldered. It took all the forenoon.

And after all that work the tractor didn't trac. Rob came into the house terribly discouraged. He said he had spent enough time on the tractor to have all his ground ready for planting. A a garage man came and worked on it for two hours without success. It would start and go for a while and then it would suddenly die down to nothing.

We had strawberry shortcake for supper, and now all of us feel stuffed. There were two quarts of strawberries on top of the big, fluffy shortcake. When we have strawberry shortcake, we like *strawberry* shortcake!

The sunset was beautiful this evening with soft yet vivid pinks and lavenders and blues. With the new green leaves of the trees stenciled against the sky, it formed a lovely changing pattern.

The children were in bed before the height of the sunset. Every minute or so, one or the other would call downstairs, "Mother, look at the sky now."

I would call back my appreciation and all would be quiet for a few minutes until the splendor became too much for them to enjoy alone, when they would call again, "Mother, look at the sky now."

Finally, when only a thin line of rose was left on the western horizon, they became quiet and dropped off to sleep.

So many times in the past I have thought how fortunate we are to be here in the country. Of course we work hard, but most people do who manage their own businesses. And in what other business can one stop in the middle of the day for an hour's rest or to talk with friends or to go somewhere one wants to go? True, chores tie us down morning and night, but during the day we are free to decide for ourselves what we will do — more or less.

But it isn't the work or lack of work that makes country living so satisfying. It is the feeling of depending on fundamental things — the earth and the sky and the good pure air, seed time and growth and harvest. The being able to go out in the sunshine with only shorts and a halter for clothes. And if people object (and they may), it's a comforting feeling to know that it's *your* land and it's nobody's business if you should happen to want to go naked. Maybe I will someday just for fun.

It isn't what you have but how you feel about what you have that makes for happiness. Farm living brings big returns in everything but money. Maybe it is because farmers as a group are too content with their lives to fight for money that they have no more. It's an interesting conjecture if nothing else.

Thursday, May 26. Cloudy. Showers. Rob thought he had the tractor all fixed this morning, and he had John hitch the horses on ahead to start the thing. It emitted many cannon-like shots and almost started several times — but not quite. They drove it down the hill from the barn, out the driveway to the road, up the road to the spring and then back to the barn. The lugs on the tractor wheels tore up the soft earth considerably around the barn. Rob is most anxious to get his potatoes planted this week and the ground is so nearly ready, it is painful, when he can't quite finish it.

The women in our part of town, the north end, are meeting tonight with Mrs. Martin Perry to make evergreen wreaths for the soldiers' graves. The wreaths will be placed after the exercises tomorrow afternoon. Most of them are made from ground pine, which grows in profusion in the woods. With its long runners, it makes beautiful garlands. The boys of the town go into the woods the day before, or that night after school and gather several bransacks full of the greenery for the women to use. From twenty-five to thirty-five wreaths are made in an evening by seven or eight women. And there are several such groups in various parts of town. We have a nice social evening together, and refreshments are served after the work is done.

Friday, May 27. Fair and warm. I went down to the Pre-Memorial program this afternoon. Just below Lewis' I saw an old man walking feebly along the road with the aid of a cane. Not recognizing him, I passed without stopping. Then I saw it was old Simon Hendricks from Athens, so I backed the car up to give him a ride.

"Which way is this car going?" he asked as I opened the car door. I thought he peered at me as if he couldn't see well. He walked weakly with his legs spread at the knees like a spider and he was shockingly dependent on his cane. He climbed with difficulty into the car.

"Some people don't like to wait for me to get in," he apologized, "it takes so long."

I assured him that there was plenty of time, but I had to repeat it, shouting, because he was so deaf. He didn't know who I was at first and I thought that was strange because he had been to our house several times since I have lived here, and he used to come over often and play his fiddle at dances. He asked me my name and he knew who I was as soon as I told him. When I stopped the car in the village in front of the town hall he asked,

"Where are we now?"

At first I thought he was joking, but I told him.

"I can't see enough to tell," he said humbly.

The children's music teacher told me that Jean's voice is improving rapidly, and she warned me to be careful of Bobby's voice because it is almost ready to change.

In the evening we went to a Health Council meeting to decide about having a Fair to raise money for health work for the children in town.

Saturday, May 28. Partly cloudy and warm. Bobby slept in his new tent last night for the first time. He kept at everyone until we helped him get the poles ready and helped put up the tent. He is so thrilled he hardly knows what to do. We put a cot in his tent and Jean found an old bench made from a split log to put in one corner. She added a homey touch by putting a vase of flowers — lilacs and violets, on the table.

Jean got up before breakfast this morning and snipped all the blossoms off the one thousand strawberry plants. It seems an awful thing to do but is necessary the first year after they are planted. She said it was especially hard when she came to a nice green strawberry and had to snip off that too.

I made rhubarb pies, a spice cake and brown bread this morning.

Bobby and his Dad hoed the vegetable garden tonight after the other work was done. Now they have gone off together on an errand in the village. It is late, past Bobby's bedtime, but we couldn't deny him the chance to pal with his father more. Both Bobby and Jean think their father is pretty special — and so do I.

Tuesday, May 31. Fair and warmer. The parts for the tractor haven't come and Rob has been trying to fix old ones so they will work. He spent most of the afternoon at the garage. Mr. Martin came over tonight to help him. They are still drawing it around hopefully. It starts occasionally, only to die down again in despair — and Rob despairs too. All this good weather going to waste and the crops waiting to be put in . . .

The children's school picnic is tomorrow if it is a good day. They are all excited about it. Bobby paid me the nicest sort of compliment tonight and I don't believe he knew it. He asked me to go to the picnic with him.

"I don't think they would want me on a school picnic," I said.

"Yes, they would," he insisted. "The teacher told us we could each bring a friend and I would like to bring you. Can't you come?"

JUNE

WEDNESDAY, *June 1. Fair and warm.* The children in Bobby's room at school hiked to the top of Bald Mountain today. They lugged all their picnic lunch up to the top of the mountain and then the fire warden told them there wasn't a safe place to build a fire there to roast the hot dogs, so they had to carry the lunch part way down the mountain again. They had lots of hot dogs, lemonade, salads, sandwiches and cake, so they must have had some load to lug around; they were happy but weary tonight.

I sat out on the portico in the lawn chair today, and a ruby-throated hummingbird came winging in so close I could have reached out my hand and touched him. He was gathering honey from the lavender columbine which grows by the wide stone steps. I could plainly see the mottled green of his back, his tiny legs drawn up so closely against his body and his beating, transparent black wings. They looked like tiny tulle veils blown out from his body by a wind.

I put the finishing touches on my flowered voile dress today.

Rob's tractor still won't work and Mr. Martin's is on the blink too. The two men are talking of going to an auction in Ware, Massachusetts, tomorrow, where three Fordson tractors are for sale. Rob is about crazy with the strain, and he said Mr. Martin was too.

Thursday, June 2. Fair and warm with increasing cloudiness toward night. This was the last day of school for the children. They both expected to pass, but until their promotion cards were in their hands they worried just a bit. They both made their grades. Next year Jean will be in the sixth grade and Bobby in the eighth. It hardly seems possible they can be growing up so fast.

Rob called Stan Martin on the telephone before five o'clock this morning. Each one was undecided whether or not to attend the auction. Stan finally came over here to discuss it further with Rob. Mr. Martin had some oats for his men to sow today and he could harrow them in with his tractor — if it went — when he returned. But if it rained before he got the oats covered he was afraid they might sprout. Thelma, his wife, and I planned to go with the men if they went, so we were on tenterhooks, too.

About seven-fifteen, they decided to go, and we left within an hour. Neither of us had much for lunches, but we made sandwiches and I had some devil's food cake frosted with maple cream. We decided to buy whatever else we needed on the way.

The trip was about seventy-five miles each way. We got there before the tractors were sold. The three Fordsons were nearly as battered-looking as ours. Two of them had no water in the radiators and Rob thought the blocks might be cracked. Anyway, they sold for all they were worth, and more. But there was a Cletrac tractor for sale, apparently in good condition — the only one they dared demonstrate — and Rob bought it. Of course, one always takes a chance buying second-hand things, but we hope it will turn out to be a good buy. Stan Martin didn't bid on one so far as I know.

Most of the people at the auction were Polish, broad-beamed and thick-legged. They *looked* less prosperous than most of our farmers in Vermont. Their features were flatter, more stolid, and one or two looked brutish.

Saturday, June 4. Cloudy. The youngsters are beginning to realize they are tired from school, although they got out early in the summer. They have shorter vacations during the year and make it up during the summer vacation.

The men hoed peas and cultivated the raspberries today.

Just as we were finishing supper, a Connecticut car drove into the dooryard. It was Rob's floriculture professor from Connecticut State College and his wife. We hadn't seen them for several years. They were on their way to Lake Sunapee for the week-end. They were here for about two hours, and we enjoyed seeing them such a lot.

Jean slept out on the porch again tonight. The mosquitoes and black flies are rather thick just now. Both children kept busy slapping until sleep finally came.

Monday, June 6. Sunny and lovely. The children helped me wash the clothes and had them out on the line early this morning. After that, they hoed the weeds out of the vegetable garden with John.

Rob was so anxious to try out his tractor that he started it early this morning. It works beautifully. He is very much pleased with it and says it is far ahead of the other one, even when it was new. He believes that if he'd had it several years ago he would be much better off now, that he could have raised more grain instead of buying it; that he could make money on his cows if he could cut down his grain costs. He hopes to finish planting his potatoes the first of this week, and he probably will if the weather holds good.

The field where he is working is fearfully dusty. When he gets off the tractor and shakes his clothes, dust rises in clouds about him. After Rob finished harrowing the land, John cleared the field of stones with the horse-drawn stone boat.

Jean is beginning to find real joy in working. She is anxious to learn how to preserve fruits and vegetables, how to make pies — especially pumpkin pies — and how to cook. She works in the garden and says it is fun. She is learning that work is a joy and a privilege. Bobby learned that before, although they will both forget it many times before they are grown . . . and afterward.

Tuesday, June 7. The children and I went to Putney over Putney Mountain this afternoon to get the tomato plants at Aiken's nursery. Mother went with us.

Coming back, I didn't know just where the Dummerston road turned off the main highway and I went past the turn about five yards before I could stop the old Buick. Two cars were behind me and I signaled my intention to back up, and they went by. Another car — with a man driving — ignored my signal and stopped short, tight behind my car, with the front of his car pointing out so I couldn't move backward.

He evidently thought he was godalmighty and that it was his duty to reprimand all erring women. He started to bawl me out in no uncertain words with such a pained, holier-than-thou note in his voice that it made me crawl to hear him.

"Don't you know how to drive?" he shouted.

Maybe I wasn't angry! And maybe I was! Even more at his voice and manner than at what he said.

"I am *trying* to back up," I told him crossly, "if you will get out of the way long enough. And where did *you* learn to drive?"

He got out of the way and it is just as well for him that he did. I hope I never see that man again!

The men worked until dark setting out tomato plants, but there are a few left to finish tomorrow.

Wednesday, June 8. Cloudy. There were showers last night, and this morning the earth and leaves and flowers look fresh and clean. The air smells good.

We had our first real meal of radishes today although we have had single ones to taste before. Our peas are budded full.

I remember that the year Bobby was born my father had peas ready to eat the ninth of June. He brought them to the hospital for me as soon as I could have them. I can still remember how good they tasted and how envious the others were. Dad's land was lighter and more sandy than ours, and gardens grew more rapidly than in the heavier soil on our farm. Dad was always doing nice, thoughtful things for people. I miss him so much now that he is gone.

The men planted potatoes in the big field below the house, today. They all got sunburns. Bobby cut potatoes all the afternoon and wore his shorts. His legs above his knees were red and sore when he got through. He pinned up his shorts in front so they wouldn't hit his sore legs.

Thursday, June 9. Fair and warm. Nice breeze blowing. This is Bobby's birthday. His thirteenth. Some of his presents, like his tent, were given to him before today, but he didn't mind. I made his favorite birthday cake — chocolate, with white icing, and decorated it with pink candy trimmings and pink and yellow birthday candles. There was only one little piece left from the big cake after we finished supper.

David Lohman spent the afternoon and evening with Bobby and stayed to supper. He made Bobby promise to eat at his house sometime. He is a nice, red-headed, freckle-faced, youngster about Bobby's age and half his size. He has a little white dog he calls Grizzly, who follows him everywhere.

Friday, June 10. Clear and warm. They didn't quite finish planting the potatoes this morning. We had an early dinner and the four of us started to Brattleboro shortly after noon.

Rob left John to run the tractor and the bush-and-bog harrow on the field across the brook.

The children went to the movies at the Paramount Theater. One of the double features had a Townshend woman in the cast, Esther Dale. The Dales own a lovely old house in Townshend village. They only come here summers now, but they used to live here all the time. I liked her in the picture. She is a fine character actress, natural and homey and kind, as she is in real life.

Saturday, June 11. Heavy showers and warmer. I awoke during the night to hear the soft sound of a gentle rain on the roof and on the leaves outside my bedroom window. A cozy sound, when one is snug and warm inside. There were showers all the morning, with a gentle mist falling in between.

The three men-folk planted potatoes in the mist, which wet through their clothes. But when a heavy shower descended, they had to give it up. Bobby took a hot bath and a cold shower and put on dry clothes, but Rob and John worked in the woodshed splitting wood until dinner time. The children filled two big woodboxes with kitchen wood outside my kitchen door, in the back kitchen.

After dinner, the sky cleared enough so the men finished getting the potatoes planted. Bobby didn't ride the planter because the soil was too mucky, and he might have been injured.

While Rob was hoeing peas in the garden after supper tonight, several neighbors dropped around and the men discussed gardens and crops and farming in general until darkness came.

Monday, June 13. A nice day with a cool breeze blowing. The cinnamon roses which grow on the south side of our house are blossomed thickly and the syringa bush is beautiful and fragrant with its star-like white flowers. The bittersweet vine, which covers the front portico, is loaded with tight little clusters of tiny white blossoms. I never saw so many flowers on it before. I hope they get pollinated this year so we'll have bitter-sweet berries this fall. They very seldom do.

I helped Bobby correct his essay for the Vermont Historical Society contest this morning. It is supposed to be in to the committee by the first of July. When he had it corrected I typed it for him.

While I was copying his essay, Bobby prepared the potatoes for dinner and picked milkweed greens. Jean made a chocolate cake. She is a good little cook but sometimes I wish she would make some other kind of cake besides chocolate!

Dr. Needham worked with Everett at his summer home all the afternoon, and I invited them to supper. They were a little late getting here and I found out the reason when they came. They had driven down to the village and the doctor brought back two quarts of ice cream, vanilla and maple walnut. I had fresh oatmeal cookies planned for supper and the ice cream was just what we needed to make the meal a success. The doctor had two and three helpings of everything so I think he must have enjoyed himself. And we enjoyed having him with us.

Bobby rode the Percheron horse, Nipper, all the afternoon, up and down the rows of potatoes, while John cultivated them.

Tuesday, June 14. Fair and sunny. A nice breeze all day. I have been reading this afternoon, articles on current topics, a short story or two, and a book review about the "mad hysterical thirties" (Christina Stead) and I feel that the madness and hysteria of the world are due in part to the fact that people forget the few fundamental laws of life and try even so to reach heaven. Here on the farm I see and hear constant signs of a Supreme Being who has time and thought for all the forms of life, and I wonder if man is as clever as he likes to believe himself to be.

I have learned that God is a great economist. He never

wastes anything. Scientists tell us that never, since the creation of this planet, has one atom of it been destroyed. Has man learned anything about these laws of nature, so much more powerful than any man-made laws?

God is systematic, too. Every little thing has a cause and a reason. The time for growth and the time for harvest, and all things should work together for good. My bittersweet vine flowers profusely, but it cannot bear fruit unless the bees pollinate the blossoms. The honeysuckles which grow beside the gray stone steps hold honey deep in their slender throats, but only the hummingbird with his long needle-like beak can get at it.

Wednesday, June 15. Clear and bright. Bobby rode on the back of the planter today, feeding the hopper. He put his foot on the iron spoke of a wheel when they stopped to fill the hopper with potatoes and forgot to take it off when they started. Only John's quick action in stopping the horses saved Bobby from having a broken leg. It is swollen and stiff and sore tonight, but he walks around on it and it should be better in the morning.

He came to the house to have it looked after; then he started back for the field. I tried to have him stay at the house and keep off it. "Do you think I'm going to stop for a little hurt like that when I'm getting paid for working?" he asked. But Rob told him that the potatoes were nearly planted and he had better rest. Nevertheless he went after the cows when it was time and did his usual chores.

Jean is trying to write stories on an old Oliver typewriter I gave the children. It is not in very good shape but it works. She started to write more on a story this evening when she noticed that Bobby had added something. She was furious at him. He had written: "P.S. I love you."

We had our first beet greens today for dinner.

Thursday, June 16. Increasing cloudiness. We saw one of the mysteries of the woods today; a tiny baby fawn. His mother had hid him under a small tree among some high ferns, in the woods. Rob almost stepped on him before he saw him. He came down from the woods to get the camera and told us it would be worth our time to see the fawn. He led the way with his effortless ground-covering gait. It looks easy but it tires most people who try to follow him. The children and I couldn't keep up without trotting every little way.

The children were ecstatic over the little fawn. We could hardly keep from touching him, he was so dear. We took pictures of him, and we had to touch him to get him in a position to photograph. We hoped his mother won't be so disturbed by the smell of humans that she will desert him.

His coat was a perfect camouflage, light brown like the dead leaves about him and spotted with white like the sunlight shining through the trees. His long slender head was flattened against the ground, his ears were laid back against his head and the only things that moved were his beautiful eyes. He was the tiniest fawn I ever saw, composed mostly of legs. He was only about eighteen inches long and a foot high.

Martin, John's brother, came down tonight to spend a couple of days with Bobby. He brought a black baby rabbit for the children.

The children have been talking about the large strawberries they found this morning. Like the stories of the largest fish always getting away, all the largest berries were eaten before they came home. Martin was describing the biggest berry he found when Jean, tired of being out-exaggerated, interrupted, "You're kind of exhausting yourself, aren't you?"

Friday, June 17. Cloudy and cool. The youngsters had a christening for their little black rabbit today. They had a long discussion as to what his (or her) name should be because they didn't know which sex it was. They compromised on the name Mickey, as that might belong to a boy or girl. Then they had a ceremony.

"We want to baptize him," Bobby said.

"No, we ought to congregate him," Jean insisted, "because we're Congregationalists."

Martin held Mickey and Bobby had a book of Bible stories to read from. Jean held the dish of water. "What shall I say?" Bobby wondered. He began, improvising as he went:

"I christen you Mickey." He dipped his hand in water and marked on the rabbit's head. "Criss . . . cross . . ." he said.

Saturday, June 18. Fair and hot. Not much breeze. The three children went strawberrying this morning as soon as the dew was off the grass. There are lots of wild strawberries in the mowing at the Woods' place. They picked about four quarts and, best of all, helped pick them over. Wild strawberries are hard to hull.

We had an enormous shortcake for supper; twice the usual size. It was loaded with all the strawberries I could make stay on; about three quarts of lusciousness, topped with thick whipped cream! I thought we could never eat it all at one meal, but we did, every crumb.

The children wanted to go swimming this afternoon, and asked me to take them down to the sheep hole. They used the argument that they deserved a reward for all their work over the strawberries. I took them. I had to go down-street after groceries and soy bean seed anyway. On the way home I had a good visit with Mother while I waited for the children to come up from the brook after their swim.

Sunday, June 19. Warm. Partly cloudy. Today was Father's Day. We wanted to do lots of *big* nice things for the children's Dad, but the farmer's dollar being what it is, we had to do the best we could with what we have. We talked it over, the three of us, and decided that Dad would like cigarettes as well as anything we could get.

Bobby did them up in a nice package, inscribed it properly so Rob would make no mistake about the purpose of the gift or the donors, and put it beside his Dad's place at the breakfast table. But the nicest thing Bobby did was to get up early, before his father was awake and do all the chores he could. He got in the cows from the night pasture, milked five of them and did the horse chores, beside sundry odd jobs about the barn.

In the meantime, Jean was getting breakfast. It all sounds heavenly. It was ... but I heard such squabbling downstairs while I was dozing in bed that I thought I'd *have* to get up quick if I wanted any pieces saved from my offspring. Bobby was trying to set the table while Jean was mixing the pancakes, and Jean was protesting violently. She wanted to be able to say that she had prepared breakfast all herself, table setting and all. (Bobby got breakfast yesterday morning and had slapped Jean away when she tried to help.) Little angels! But I wouldn't swap 'em for anything.

Monday, June 20. Fair and warmer. Mary Martin came over this afternoon to have me type her essay for the Windham County Historical Society. It is about the Twin Houses, their house and ours, which were built by the Brigham brothers before the year 1800. She told of the good-natured competition between the two brothers to have each house a gem of its kind, and their labor over hand-carving woodwork in each house. All the square-headed nails and hand-wrought hardware were made in a blacksmith shop in Harmonyville, a part of Townshend. The wide pine boards were sawed in the first sawmill in town, located about a mile from our house, and the potato whiskey served at our house when it was a tavern was made in a whiskey mill not much more than a stone's throw away. One year a farmer in Brookline brought over one thousand bushels of potatoes to be made into whiskey. He must have had some high old times that winter. I wonder if there were enough potatoes left for the family to eat. Local legend doesn't state.

Wednesday, June 22. Partly cloudy. I saw the bobolink who has been giving us so much pleasure with his singing (at least, one

of the bobolinks). He was in the tall grass near the house. I got quite close to him before he flew away. Bobolinks have their nests down in the old barnyard in the tall grasses each year. I like what Thoreau says of their song:

"It is as if he [the bird] touched his harp with a vase of liquid melody, and when he lifted it out the notes fell like bubbles from the strings . . . away he launches, and the meadow is all bespattered with melody."

Bobby helped Jean with the dishes this morning so she could help him weed the garden. "You know," Jean remarked, "Last year I didn't like to work much, but this year I think it is fun — all except washing dishes. I don't believe I'll *ever* like to do that."

Rob and John finished getting in the hay this morning. John and Bobby got most of it in yesterday, while Rob was finishing the tractor.

An inspector from the Vermont Department of Agriculture, Division of Markets, called this morning to inspect our syrup for density and color. We use the Vermont quality label on our syrup so they check up every year or so. Our syrup passed all right as we knew it would; we take plenty of pains to make it that way. The inspector said it seemed good to find syrup with the proper density. A lot he had tested had been too thin. He said he never realized how many different flavors maple syrup could have.

The inspector told us that practically all the best flavored syrup now comes from trees on high land. He attributed it in part to the ravages of the tree caterpillar and partly to the warmer temperature which hits the valleys before it does the high land.

David Lohman's mother sent me a night letter which was telephoned up this morning by Western Union. She asked me to look after David until she arrives. David will come over tomorrow morning when Joe leaves. David said, "She doesn't think I am old enough to look after myself." I told him I would feel the same way if it were Bobby being left alone. I know he would be all right but just the same I would want to be sure. . . .

Thursday, June 23. Fair and hot. Today has been intensely hot, with practically no wind stirring. The earth is dry and we need rain badly.

David came early this morning. His little white dog, Grizzly, came with him. The three children have played and worked very nicely together for the most part. More difficulties always arise when there is an odd number.

Rob's brother John came over from Springfield, Vermont, this morning to measure the barn roof. It must be re-roofed this summer. They figured that it will cost almost seven hundred dollars. It seems an awful price to pay for one roof but it is an immense barn, with a hip roof. The barn is 120 ft. long and 40 ft. wide. Galvanized roofing would be cheaper than shingles and much easier to lay and would probably last longer.

"Why did your grandfather ever make a barn with such a large roof surface?" I asked Rob.

"When that barn was built, the whole of it didn't cost much more than the roof would cost today," he explained. "In 1903 materials were much cheaper compared to the farm income. Father said it cost about $1500. They cut logs from the farm, bought nails and paid for sawing. . . .

"Horace Gale built his big barn in 1906. He said when he started building it he didn't know where the money was coming from, but by the time it was built it was all paid for — and he roofed it with slate. He doesn't know to this day just how much the barn cost, he kept no expense account. He sold a few more cows than he really wanted to that summer; he sold ten cows altogether, but it didn't drain his resources any appreciable amount. The cows were good, but not purebreds or of any special line. Fifty dollars apiece today, they wouldn't bring a 'drop in the bucket' compared to the cost of building that barn."

John Follett stayed to dinner and he plans to come over again tomorrow. Jean baked a chocolate cake for dinner. There were only two small pieces left. David told her that if she would bake another cake just like it, he would furnish the materials. He wished his mother could bake a cake like it. (Wouldn't his mother love that?) I told Jean she could bake another one for supper if she wanted to. Spurred on by his praise, she concocted a new dish. She picked strawberries to go on top of the chocolate cake. Then she found there weren't enough to cover it thickly so she had the boys help her pick more. Wild strawberries are more delicious than any tame ones that ever grew, and mixed with sugar, I think they would blend with almost any dish. None of us ever heard of a strawberry chocolate cake but we didn't need to be told twice. Every crumb disappeared quickly.

Jean got all the supper. She made a delicious potato salad and garnished it attractively with lettuce and radish slices.

Friday, June 24. Herbert Waters, who is going to do the woodcuts for this journal if it is published, came up today to see what our farm looks like. He is a quiet, comfortable person, and I enjoyed sharing our farm and the land around it with an artist who can catch its feeling in a way that seems to me more dramatic than words.

The school nurse and I spent the afternoon visiting parents. It has been another interesting experience. As always, the indomitable courage and independence of our people impresses me. Yes, we have the spongers too, but they are a small minority. The thing I like about our system is that it strives to help people to help themselves. Many of the New Deal dependents would be put to shame if they could see the willing sacrifices and careful planning of the people, to give their children the advantages of good health and good education.

Saturday, June 25. Still very hot and fair. A climax came in the relations between David and the other children today and I had to step in and arbitrate. Ever since David began to come here he has tried to impress the others with his own superior brains, and they don't like it. It is his father's fault more than David's. His father is constantly saying how brilliant David is and how far advanced for his age.

There is no question but that David is smart and gets good marks, but he is in Bobby's grade in school and is the same age as Bobby and I consider that Bobby is a normal child. Anyway, David shouldn't be spoiled by it.

It was a piling up of little incidents that caused the storm. Bobby has to work and David doesn't. David said, "I don't have to work; I am smart and smart people don't have to work."

That made Bobby boil. Then David began to correct everything both children did, telling them that they were wrong but if they would do it as *he* said. . . .

I heard the loud angry voices on the lawn and went out. I had been keeping close track of the way things were going for some time. I told David that he had his values mixed, that while he was here he was just as important as the other children but no more so; that there were three of them and it was only fair that each of the three should be treated equally, that he couldn't have his way any more than his share. And, I added (maybe I shouldn't have) that I had been told that he was a spoiled child, and he was acting it.

That set him thinking. His aunts had repeatedly told me how he was spoiled at home. He went up in the maple tree on the lawn and sat there thinking soberly for a long time. I wondered if I had said too much. When I went out I was careful to show by my manner that the punishment was over and that was all there was to it; I held no grudge. When it came time for Bobby to get the cows, he asked David if he wanted to go with him.

"Uh-uh, not me," David said, shaking his head.

But later, David was up in the barn, helping, and he has been the nicest boy imaginable ever since, helpful and willing.

The boys had a lot of fun together this evening out on the

grass in front of the tent. It was cool there in the dusk and a steady breeze was blowing. Jean went to bed but I let the boys stay up, for David still hoped his folks would come.

About nine, he decided they wouldn't arrive and went to bed. And then they came. They had driven slowly because Mr. Lohman still felt ill. David was so glad to see them that he almost forgot to take his little dog when he went home with them.

Sunday, June 26. Rainy and cooler. The heat wave broke last night. Our bedroom is on the south of the house, and it was hot when we went to bed so we opened the window by the bed. (There are four windows in the bedroom and a fireplace and three doors and that window is usually left shut except in hot weather.) The wind blew in little gusts over our hot bodies. Soon we pulled up the sheet and it billowed in the wind like waves on a lake; then we needed a light blanket. We slept deeply and sweetly, after we had watched hundreds of fireflies lighting the grass in the meadow by the barn. They are such glowing, friendly little things, they make one drowsy in spite of oneself.

I woke about two o'clock to the welcome sound of rain. We put down the windows on the south side of the house, where the wind was blowing the rain in, and went back to sleep.

Monday, June 27. Rainy and cool. We had a surprise tonight. The school nurse phoned to say that one town poor family has earned ten dollars to apply on a tonsil operation for their child. The family has been on relief for several years, first because of real necessity in time of illness and then afterward apparently because it was comfortable to be looked after without personal effort. This spring the town fathers tried the old John Smith idea: Those who won't work can't eat. One man expressed it:

"I'm glad they (the family) are interested in something at last."

Wednesday, June 29. Clear and warmer. A beautiful day after the rain.
Rob went to an auction at the Black farm in Brattleboro today
with Royal Cutts and Stanley Martin. They left about ten and
were gone all day. Rob bought a potato digger for thirty-five
dollars. He thinks it is a good bargain.

He says he doesn't wonder they couldn't make the farm pay.
They had ten men during sugaring to look after two thousand
buckets.

We had dinner early. The children spent the afternoon with
Mary Martin. It was her thirteenth birthday. They had a grand
time.

And I went to Brattleboro to a County Health Council meeting, at Mr. R.M. Bradley's estate. There was a luncheon on the
lawn. His daughter, Mrs. Gamble, was Mr. Bradley's hostess. It
was a delightful occasion and afterward, we had a very interesting meeting. Mr. Bradley was presented with a plaque express-
ing the appreciation and affection of all the people who have
worked with him during the thirty-eight years he has been a
trustee of the Thompson Fund and administrator of county
health. He is a grand old man.

Nearly all the towns in the county were represented and
each town gave interesting and vivid accounts of the health
work done in its community. Incredible hardships have to be
overcome, and a few parents still need rousing from their
lethargy concerning the health of their children.

While driving to Brattleboro I picked up a man and a woman
who were walking into town, carrying a basket of clothes between them. They are brother and sister and they live about
eight miles outside of Brattleboro. Since they walk to town
several times each week, they are a familiar sight to residents
for miles around. If they don't get a ride, the round trip means
sixteen miles of walking on hard blacktop road, with cars
whizzing by from both directions.

"You have lots of courage," I told them.

"Ye-es," the sister admitted hesitatingly. "But we manage all right and people are usually very kind."

And she went on to tell of kind people who had carried them "all the way home from Brattleboro" some days. She told how deeply grateful they were for all the favors done them, but she never spoke of the hardships of their lives. The brother, I know, is mentally deficient and she has to plan all their work.

They do washings for several people in Brattleboro and carry the washings back and forth over the eight miles, often on foot, with the basket hung between them. They tap nearly two hundred sugar maples each spring and lug all the sap by hand from the trees to their small evaporator, where it is boiled down to syrup. In berry season they carry berries to town.

"We used to have a horse," they told me, "but he died."

They didn't say that they couldn't afford to buy another. The man needed a shave, but they were neat and clean and the woman's face shone with the fullness of living. I thought of the Bible text, "If ye have faith as a grain of mustard seed. . . ."

Thursday, June 30. Fair and cool. A brisk breeze blowing. The temperature was forty degrees at five this morning.

I was dreadfully tired when I got home last night and went to bed immediately after supper. I woke up several hours later feeling queer and uneasy. I couldn't understand why. I turned over several times and couldn't go to sleep; that strange feeling persisted. Finally the trouble dawned on me. Heavens, I was supposed to stop at the Chambers' and tell Mrs. Chambers there would be no tonsil clinic held tomorrow and I had completely forgotten it. What if the two boys who were to have their tonsils out should get to the hospital, all keyed up for the operation, and the superintendent should tell them there was a mistake?

The more I thought about it the worse it seemed. I lay in bed in the dark and wondered how I could get word to them. They have no telephone and none of their near neighbors in the village have telephones. The nearest one is in the home of an elderly couple who would be in bed long ago and wouldn't get up until long after the boys might be in Brattleboro.

I decided that the only thing to do was to get up at five in the morning and go down to the village and tell them. I wasn't looking forward to the job; they might rightly feel cross at my forgetfulness. I slept fitfully until about two hours before I needed to get up and then fell into a heavy sleep. Promptly at five I awoke, dressed hurriedly, got into the car and went down.

I got Mrs. Chambers out of bed. She had telephoned from her neighbor's house late the evening before, to the school nurse, so she already knew the clinic was postponed, but I believe she felt better when she knew I hadn't willfully neglected to tell her.

She invited me into the house and we had a nice early morning chat, she in her bathrobe and slippers which she had thrown on hurriedly in answer to my knock. As I was ready to leave, she stopped me. She wanted me to see the bureau she had bought at an auction a few days before.

It was a nice bureau, with plenty of room, but the most interesting thing was the story about it. She bought the bureau and had a neighbor bring it home in his light truck. She carried the drawers into the house and laid them on the kitchen table while she helped the neighbor carry the bureau into the house. When she took the old newspapers out of the drawers she found, between the sheets, three large, old-style one-dollar bills. The people who had owned the bureau had died. They had probably slipped the money in between the sheets of newspaper sometime, for a small nest egg, and had then forgotten it.

"It's like something you read about in stories," she said.

A few of our currants are ripe and Jean picked about two cups full. I put them in sour cream pancakes for supper. They tasted scrumptious, smothered in maple syrup.

JULY

SUNDAY, *July 3. Cold.* Dr. Needham and four guests came up to his house last night for over the Fourth. He was over here early this morning for milk, and stayed to chat. He brought over their ice cream freezer for us to use.

Sister, the mare, has a lame foot and she can hardly walk on it. This morning Rob called the veterinary, Dr. Hopkins. Fortunately, he was planning to visit the Horse Farm so he didn't have to make a special trip. There was another veterinary with him and they agreed that Sister must have sprained her foot. That means we cannot use her for a few days — right in haying.

Our new minister has come and he began his pastorate Sunday. I believe we will like him and his wife very much. Mr. Marsh has been pastor at Enfield, Massachusetts, which is to be flooded this fall. Enfield has had much publicity lately over the radio and in newspapers. The flood dam was called a 1940 project, but it will be completed ahead of time.

The flood dam project and fate of Enfield brings home to us

what might happen to Townshend. For two years government surveyors have repeatedly surveyed the West River valley and talked of building a dam in the West River below Newfane, the town below us, which would virtually wipe out Townshend, West Townshend, Newfane and Brookline. So far as we can ascertain, the dam as proposed would do little good in case of a flood but would be a source of cheap power to some power company.

All the people in the valley and in surrounding towns are fighting it and will continue to do so. The new law recently enacted by Congress, which attacks the state's right to protect its own resources, causes some alarm. Vermont may be a small state but, as Calvin Coolidge once said, "If Democracy should languish and perish from the rest of the world, it could all be replenished from the little state of Vermont" — in spite of voting Republican.

"We might have some more Green Mountain Boys," one stalwart Vermonter said, "if they try to come in and take away what is ours."

Monday, July 4. Cold and dark, extremely chilly for this time of year.

The youngsters arose early this morning and appropriately started the day off with a bang. Several days ago Bobby made long fuses with twine and chemicals from his chemistry set. They fastened these fuses to the fuse on the firecrackers and lit the long end farthest from the firecracker. It was different, and I heartily approved the idea because I thought it was safer. There was only a moderate supply of fireworks but, used carefully, they lasted all day.

In the evening we went down to Mother's, and the children lit sparklers on the lawn where everyone could enjoy them.

Tuesday, July 5. Fair and warm. Nice breeze. After my washing was done this morning, Jean and I picked currants. They are nice and large this year. They are none too ripe but we have to race with the birds. They like ripe currants too. It was amusing as well as exasperating to hear the birds scold us for interfering with their berries. We picked four quarts. There are lots more, as soon as they are ready.

Wednesday, July 6. Clear and warm. Bobby and Jean each came to me separately this morning and told me they were glad I made them go to bed early last night. I reminded them that they hadn't been too gracious about it then, and that so far as I was concerned I wouldn't care when they went to bed, but I was thinking of their welfare. You cannot discuss things with them when they are tired, you just have to tell them what to do. For then they can't reason, they just feel. Jean said, "I am glad I have a good father and mother who make me do what is right." I'm glad they feel that way now, and hope we can keep their confidence through their adolescence.

Often I doubt my wisdom in dealing with their problems. I feel I need more patience and understanding. But one thing the children know, that I make no claim to superior wisdom, merely claim more experience. And if I don't know a thing, I tell them so and we work it out together. I can think of several of my sainted ancestors who would think it was "criminal" to do such things. How ironic, that by the time we parents really have learned how to bring up children, those children have grown up and there is no more need of our liberal knowledge in one of the most necessary fields of education. And our children will be just as rabid as we were about their right to bring up their individual families in their own way.

A barn swallow's nest was taken down from the eaves of the barn today. There were five little birds in the nest. All the children took turns getting worms and feeding the little birds, with their funny cavernous mouths. I warned the youngsters against overfeeding the baby birds, but they thought they were hungry because they kept opening their mouths. Bobby looked at them just before he went to bed tonight and four of them were dead. Both children feel terribly to think they had a part in the tragedy. They vow it won't happen again. But the birds were cunning, crowded into a nest which seemed about big enough for one, with those wide yellow beaks opening again and again against their dun-colored feathers. Those incredible mouths! It was like watching clowns at a circus, only funnier.

The men have been haying all day today and most of the hay that's cut is cured and in the barn. It smells sweet and pungent when we go inside the wide barn doors. Rob mowed more after supper until darkness had fallen so deeply he couldn't see.

Our red roses are in bloom now. Jean loves them because "they have such a strong sweetness of a smell," she says.

Thursday, July 7. Clear in the morning. Partly cloudy in the afternoon. The men have been busy getting the hay all day, first turning it, then raking it, then loading it onto the hay wagon and carrying it into the barn, where it is put in the mow with the hay fork. The field in front of the house, where they are working, is too rough and small to use the hay loader.

Bobby is learning to drive the horses and to tread down the hay on the load so it balances evenly. That leaves the two men on the ground to pitch the hay onto the load.

Anna Ela (who owns the Morgan Horse Farm near us) and the girl who rides her horses to exercise them stopped this afternoon while riding two of their young geldings. We discussed the coming Townshend Fair in all its phases.

The sky looks like rain tonight and the farmers who have hay out are nervous about it.

Saturday, July 9. Fair and hot in the morning. Scattered showers in the afternoon. The young stock got out of our hill pasture, where they are kept during the summer and went down to the Morgan Horse Farm. Rob, Bobby and Jean went after them, brought them back to the farm, and then drove them back on the hill. It took them most of the morning. On their way, they saw a fawn and its mother. It was much larger than the one we saw in the woods a few weeks ago.

Jean and I picked currants most of the morning. There are still many more to pick. Part of them I will sell. The director's meeting at the milk plant was this afternoon and we went with Rob. We hadn't much money but we pooled our resources and went just the same, the children were to be paid back as soon as the milk check comes.

We had a grand afternoon. The movie, "Tom Sawyer," was playing at the auditorium for just the one day. The children loved it. They wished they could see it over again so they could remember every scene better, but that was out of the question.

Sunday, July 10. Fair and hot. I started to get out of bed this morning when my small daughter came bouncing up the stairs. "Oh, Mother," she said. "Don't get up, *please*, I have a surprise for you." I climbed back into bed, gratefully. Jean brought my breakfast upstairs to me. Now I have breakfast in bed so seldom that it is a treat. And it was so nicely prepared and arranged. The children did the dishes and Bobby vacuumed the living room before I got up. But then, how I had to hurry to get around before church. I'm afraid that if it hadn't been for the children I would have back-slid and stayed home.

Tuesday, July 12. Showers all day. A rattling thundershower at night. This has been a busy day and a lot has been accomplished.

I have canned all day. I finished at seven-fifteen tonight; Swiss chard and beet greens and peas and currant juice. Thirty-five cans. And that's a lot of greens and peas and currants. They take plenty of time to prepare. If anyone doubts it, he ought to be made to pick a bushel of peas from the garden, sit down and shell them, then wash and blanch them and put them in cans and process them for three hours.

I looked around for enough of something easy to prepare

which would fill three more cans, but I couldn't find a thing. Then I could have boasted that I had put up fifty cans in two days. Why does fifty of anything sound so much larger than forty-seven?

The children were good to help, by fits and starts. They shelled part of the peas but they got tired and wanted to go over to Browns'.

Sammy-dog found a woodchuck this morning. He couldn't get it out of its hole alone so he barked frantically for help. Rob went to help him and found such a cute baby woodchuck that he brought it home to show the children and me.

When the Lohmons stopped for their milk this evening, Rob asked them jokingly, "Want something for breakfast?"

"It's alive," Bobby said.

"It's a woodchuck — a baby one," said Jean.

The Lohmons were interested, but not hungry.

All five us played croquet out on the side lawn this evening until large drops of rain began to fall and thunder started to roll. Then the children went to bed and I was about to go when Ruth and her young man came. We had a nice visit while the storm gathered force outside.

The wind came up and lightning flashed close by. Large hailstones beat against the window panes and came down the wide mouth of the chimney into the fireplace. A few bounced out onto the floor. They were large and hard, some of them as big as marbles. Suddenly there was a blinding flash and then darkness. The electricity was gone again and probably the transformer. I lit candles and called to the children to reassure them and myself. I wanted to know they were all right, Bobby in his tent outdoors and Jean upstairs in her room.

Bobby said, "I was scared but Sammy was scareder; he crawled under my bed and shivered and wouldn't even wag his tail when I said, 'good dog'."

Ruth and a friend of hers are taking orders for home-cooked foods and are selling them at a fair profit. She said they were doing quite well. She asked for suggestions for the grab bag at the Guild sale later this month. Rob said, "I know a good 'grab' for you," and he left the room in a mysterious manner.

He came back with the box containing the woodchuck, carefully covered.

"Will you grab?" he asked Ruth.

Knowing him, she wouldn't. The woodchuck obligingly clacked his teeth while we watched him.

Wednesday, July 13. Fair and hot. Rob has left the job of picking and marketing the peas to Everett and Jed Hill. They are to have a third of the crop for their work. They ought to make a good thing out of it. We will probably have more than a hundred bushels of peas. I wish we had time to do it ourselves but it is out of the question just now, in the midst of haying outdoors and canning in the house. Jed picked peas for over five hours today — two bushels. He should have done it in an hour.

Rob and John built a new hay rack for the wagon yesterday during the rain. They used it this afternoon getting in hay.

Thursday, July 14. Showers in the afternoon. Last night we had some excitement. The children and I had gone to bed and Rob was talking to Royal downstairs in the kitchen, when we heard what we thought were shots. The noise continued and we decided it sounded like firecrackers. It came from the direction of the road which leads to town.

Then John came home. On his way up the hill he had almost run into a car parked in the middle of the road with all its lights out except for one taillight. The people in the car started on, pulled down the back curtain of their sedan, and turned into Dr. Needham's driveway, to let John by.

We watched the sedan and saw it back into the barway at the foot of the last hill, leading into our potato field. There they lit more firecrackers. They were talking and making quite a lot of noise, and we decided they were young people out on a party.

Rob and Royal watched them from the butternut tree in front of the house. Finally, they decided to walk down across the potato field and see what was going on. Sammy sensed what they planned, and he ran ahead of them down to the parked car and began barking. The men got nearly to the barway when those inside the car started to get out and Rob and Royal squatted down among the potatoes, so they wouldn't be seen. Someone began firing rocks at Sammy and he started back toward Rob, trying to keep from being hit. A rock landed right in front of Rob.

He jumped to his feet angrily and started for the car. "You — this and that —" he yelled, "What do you think you are doing?"

The occupants of the car piled in their automobile and were off like a shot, down the road and away. Rob and Royal climbed back up the hill, got into our car and followed until they got to the main road and found the car had gone north. They thought they recognized one of the people in the car as a young hoodlum from the village. The outside edges of the numberplate were hard to see, the way the taillight shone on it, but the men got all but two numbers of it and were nearly sure of those.

We didn't think the episode serious enough to report until the next morning when Rob met Mr. Smith down at Father's when he took the milk. Mr. Smith was sure the first of the shots the night before were fired from a gun — an automatic — and the firecrackers were set off afterward. (The young hoodlum Rob thought he recognized owns such a weapon.) Later, during the night, the black sedan returned and Mr. Smith heard some shooting in the alders below his house. He was worried enough so he searched the alders and sent his sons to look up his young cattle. He could see no trace of anything being dragged out to the road, although they might have carried something out. A few farmers nearby have lost some of their young stock and they are wondering if they have been taken by some gang working in this section.

The game warden came up this afternoon, and we checked through his book of automobile registrations without learning anything definite. We are keeping a careful watch, although we hope they won't return.

Rob mowed hay this morning. It dried well and they got most of it into the barn before the first shower struck here. In fifteen minutes more all the hay would have been in, worse luck.

Friday, July 15. Sunny and comfortably warm. Nice day. Our mare, Sister, stepped in a woodchuck hole yesterday and today is so lame she can hardly walk. We need her badly, right in haying. It seems as if we ought to be able to have a run of good luck for a while, soon; we've had plenty of the other kind in spite of our hard work.

I took the children down to choir rehearsal tonight and on our way home we saw a deer in the raspberries. I drove up to the house as fast as I could to get Rob to shoot it. He was busy dusting the potatoes and couldn't hear when we called to him. Jean ran through a row of potato plants until she reached him. He walked back to the barn, put up the hand duster he was using, came down to the house, where Bobby had his 38-55 loaded and ready for him. We got into the car and I drove him down to the corner, where he slid out of the car and I drove along. The deer was still waiting.

It was dusk and hard to see the sights on the gun, and Rob was disgusted with himself that it took four shots to bring the deer down. It was a young buck with his horns in the velvet, a six-pointer. The game warden came soon after we called him. Deer have damaged the raspberries terribly.

Saturday, July 16. Sunny and cool. An ideal summer day. Rob and I went to the Balls' farm late this afternoon to get Mrs. Jenkins and take her to the village to stay with her sister.

She hadn't been off the farm since last November — eight

months ago, even though the farm is less than a mile from the main road, for she was unable to walk. I have always wanted to go to the Balls' but Rob wouldn't let *me* drive up there and when he went he always carried a load. But this time there was only Mrs. Jenkins to bring down.

One would never dream there was a road leading somewhere, as we turned off the main road and started up the hill. So few people passed that way in automobiles that the road was grown up with grass and thickly hedged in by trees and underbrush. Yet I know that many people go to the Balls', walking up and then down again, for they are interesting people, warmhearted and friendly. The rough road wound up through the woods, with branches from the trees touching the car on either side. It seemed we had entered a different world, and the car was a thing out of place. We should be riding in an ox-cart or, at best, a buggy.

And then, around a sharp turn in the road, a gray, weather-beaten farmhouse came into sight. It was nearly smothered with vines and looked old, old, as though it had been there forever, and I had the strangest feeling of having stepped back in time fifty years or more.

We stopped the car by the back door and got out. Wooden wash tubs set on wooden standards stood on the ground outside the covered entry, half filled with dirty water left from the washing on the line. Bright, beautiful begonias were planted in beds close to the house, protected from the wandering hens by a low woven-wire fence stretched around the flower beds. Friendly people, three or four of them, came out of the house through the kitchen door to greet us.

An old, old lady sat inside by an open window. She leaned close to the screen and demanded to know who was there. Everyone stopped and listened to that voice and obeyed its summons.

"Who is it? Who are you?"

Myrtie, the old lady's daughter answered.

117

"It's the Folletts. You know who they are."

"Yes, I know the Folletts and they have always been well spoken of. I have known a number of them. I am ninety-one years old," she said proudly. "And what did you say your name was?" she asked me.

Myrtie explained that I am Rob Follett's wife, and with subtle flattery the old lady peered up into my face as I stood by the window and remarked, "Well, I'm glad he has a good one."

I looked and looked at this remarkable old woman about whom I have heard so much and around whom legends are already being built. She is slim and small and has a shock of vibrant, curly white hair, cut short and parted in the middle, with bangs falling on her forehead; I never before saw such live-looking hair on an old person. Her blue eyes looked keen and sharp, but Myrtie said she is almost blind and can only see out of one corner of her right eye. Myrtie said her mother used to write a good many letters and she might have injured her eyes that way. She kept a soft towel in her hands and continually wiped her mouth and eyes with it.

Her dress and Myrtie's fitted loosely, and the prints looked like the old-fashioned calico in the pieces in Great-Grandmother's quilt. Myrtie's hair was done up in a loose knot on the top of her head. But it was Myrtie's face which one noticed. It was sweet and animated and beautiful in a tired sort of way. Her features are lovely now, for her bones are fine, and I would like to have seen her when she was young. But pushed away back, behind the animation, was a sadness which was haunting, especially when one knew her story. . . . But her mother was speaking.

"I wish I had some of the cheeses your grandmother used to make," she told Rob.

"It wasn't his grandmother, it was his great-grandmother," Myrtie corrected her.

"Oh, well," she shrugged delicate shoulders. "Eliza used to make awfully good cheeses."

"She never got things mixed until this summer," Myrtie apologized. "She was awfully sick early this spring and she hasn't been the same since."

And thus began a conversation which was a weird shuttle between people who lived years ago when she was young and the younger generations. Before she was through I didn't wonder she got mixed when she tried to keep five or six generations of families distinct in her mind. Eliza Follett died in 1900, but to Mrs. Ball she seemed closer than my generation did.

Then Myrtie began to talk of her two brothers and Rob's father and how it made her feel like crying to see them so feeble and old-looking. I turned to look more closely at "the boys," as she called her brothers. They did look nearly as old as their mother, bent and wrinkled and thin, and there was something in their faded eyes . . . a hopelessness, a fear, as though life were slipping away from them without even memories to hold them back and hearten them in the shadows.

None of the three children had married and I recalled some of the stories I'd heard; how their mother had always enjoyed poor health and how she had spent most of her life in bed. But her spells were usually brought on when her authority was threatened or whenever her children wanted to do something which might loosen them from her will. Myrtie was engaged to marry for years but her mother wouldn't let her marry the man. She needed to have Myrtie sleep with her and how could she if she were married? And what would she do without Myrtie to care for her all the time? The mere suggestion always sent her into a bad spell. After all, with her poor health, she wouldn't live long and couldn't Myrtie wait until she was dead? It wasn't much to ask, just a year or two longer, maybe not that.

And so Myrtie and John waited. And Myrtie was thirty, and then forty, and fifty came and still her mother was as well as she had been when her daughter was fifteen and had taken over the burdens of the household. Once or twice a week I used to see John and Myrtie ride down to the village in the old buggy behind the bay driving horse. John lived with them then and helped the "boys" with the farm work. Even then, young as I was, I was struck by their expressions; a blending of frustration and longing — and a little hope, which dwindled as the years passed. And then John died, after waiting almost a lifetime for the only girl he ever loved.

Mrs. Ball is treated like a beloved child who must be watched and tended and guarded from all unpleasant things, but she gave me the impression of having a store of resilient strength, even more than her hard-working children. Myrtie confided that she herself is not at all well. She has a bad heart trouble and she sometimes has fainting spells. But her sweetness and selflessness were like bright banners carrying her along.

She told me that they came to this farm fifty years ago last May. She took me up to the barn, through the barn-floor and out into the barnyard to show me where they could look to see lights in their neighbor's windows at night. It was away across the valley and on another hill to the east of them, where another lonely farmhouse stood. Then she showed me the rocks in the barnyard, worn smooth with age, where she and her brothers used to play when they were children, and her special rock which she called her chair. Sure enough, there was a worn depression in the rock just large enough for a not-too-big child to sit comfortably.

The farm is cocked upon a sharply slanting hillside and is beginning to be claimed again by fast-growing vegetation. Two huge piles of manure reach in conical heaps up the outside of the barn to the high barn windows, from which it is thrown when the stable is cleaned. It must have been accumulating there for more than a year, and it would have put new life into the thinning soil.

Mrs. Ball's husband was a Civil War veteran. He was captured by the Southern army and sent to the prison in Andersonville. Conditions there, as everyone knows, were terrible. Mr. Ball became so ill that prison authorities freed him, with a companion, because the two were expected to die anyway, and it might save digging a hole to bury them.

Somehow, the two men lived and they slowly worked their way North and came home. Mr. Ball never recovered from the effects of the war, although he married and had three children and brought them to this farm in Vermont, surrounded and hidden by forests and nearly inaccessible. He must have wanted to get as far away as possible from everything which might remind him of his war experiences. He died years ago.

But people come to them now. They nearly always have company, and someone, usually some old person, is always staying with them. Myrtie told of that feeble old man, Simon Hendricks, walking over from Athens and up that hill, to bring her two baskets of fresh blueberries. There are only a few ripe yet and he knew they would be a treat. He is almost blind and extremely deaf and so feeble he can hardly navigate. I don't know how he managed to get there and Myrtie wondered, too.

Myrtie said she wanted to give him something in return, but she didn't know what she had to give him until she thought of her butter. She remembered how he liked her butter; there were only three people's butter that he would eat and hers was one of them, so she wrapped up a pound for him to take home. She said she didn't know how she ever thought of it, for she had a lot of company the day he came and she was very busy. But after I had talked with her, I wasn't surprised. She is that kind of a person.

Myrtie very rarely goes off the hill now, since John died, and her mother hasn't been away from home for years and years. So they slip back into the ways of the past more and more. They have no so-called modern inventions and would probably feel lost with them. Sometimes, on clear quiet nights, they can hear the traffic going past on the main road, the sounds muted and softened by distance. It is near enough for them. The very atmosphere around them *feels* old-world.

It's the strangest sensation! When I started up that hill I felt like a normal adult able to cope with my world, but after spending an hour with them I felt like Alice in Wonderland, growing smaller and smaller and younger all the time. It was that parade of people coming to life by the Balls' imaginations, after having been dead for many years. Rob and I were the shadowy figures of future generations while Great-Grandmother Eliza and her children were still inhabiting the earth. It was with a shock of surprise that I remembered that we were parents, Rob and I, with half-grown offspring of our own.

We brought Mrs. Jenkins safely down to her sister's where, for a few brief summer months, she will live in our present-day world. But when it comes fall, she will no doubt go back to keep the old folks company, where time stands still even though people grow old.

Sunday, July 17. Sunny and hot. Sister, the mare, is much better this morning. They are going to try working her today. Some time during last night she unsnapped her bridle from the halter and sauntered outdoors to see what she could see and eat her fill of good green grass.

Bobby said that he woke up out of a sound sleep and heard queer crunching sounds outside his tent. He was somewhat startled but he managed to climb out of bed and peer carefully out the left side of his tent, which was in shadow, while the other side was bathed in bright moonlight. He had heard that discretion was the better part of valor. And there was Sister, contentedly chewing grass. Bobby led her back into the barn and after he had hitched her he put the rope across the end of the stall, back of her. It is always supposed to be fastened back of her for Sister is noted for her roving feet, but someone had forgotten to do it.

All of us went to church this morning. It was stifling hot there, even with the windows open. After dinner Ruth and her young man drove up in his car and took the children to the river for a swim.

That left Rob and me alone together for a delicious, lazy afternoon. It so seldom happens that it is a treat and a novelty, when we both have nothing to do but enjoy one another's company. So far as I am concerned, all eternity would be too short a time for that.

Monday, July 18. Rainy and warm. A large part of Burbee's mill burned today. Rob and John went down to fight fire about seven-thirty this morning. They didn't stop to finish their breakfast, just grabbed a cup of coffee, a slice of toast apiece, and were gone. I wanted to go and so did the children. It seemed cruel for me to run off into excitement and leave them behind, and I didn't want them to go into too much danger — not yet — so the three of us stayed behind and kept ourselves informed of the happenings by telephone.

The men came back at ten-thirty and told us all about it. Rob was in the hottest, hardest place he could find, as usual. He and a few others worked to save the drying room, which joined the blazing inferno. When he came home his lungs were sore from the smoke, and he shut all the doors in the house because he was so cold. It must have been eighty-five degrees in the kitchen, but where he had been the temperature had gone away above a hundred. He sat on the hearth of the stove and shivered. Tonight, he is apparently all right and didn't catch cold.

This afternoon I went with him to Brattleboro to get a load of grain. I went to the Stephen Daye Press, but Marion was away.

I put up eight cans of venison today, between excitements. The pressure cooker had to be watched, too, so it wouldn't blow up.

Friday, July 22. Hard rain all morning, cloudy all day. Some of the large telephone peas are ready to pick. I tried to get word to the boys that they were ready. The boys were out but Father delivered the message.

After supper they came up to tell us they weren't going to

take the job. Just like that — and the peas ready to be market-ed! We had been warned that Jed would probably back out but I had hoped that Everett could market them with Bobby's help, but he didn't feel able to. Jed said he had decided that it wouldn't pay, but I imagine he thought he might have to work a little harder than he wanted to. He talked about taking two days to get rid of a load, one day to pick them and another day to sell them. Why hadn't he told us that before the peas were ready for picking?

It made me angry. He had hemmed and hawed so much about wanting a job and when he had a chance at one he up and left it. I told him a few things we all had been aching to tell him for a long time, although I didn't really let myself get started. Now we are left in the midst of haying and canning with the whole crop of peas to dispose of, and that means just one thing. I will have to sell them, with what help the children can give, and I hate the job. I could choke Jed cheerfully. And then he had the nerve to want me to stop and cut his hair and he acted surprised when I refused.

There was another Fair meeting tonight and quite a lot was accomplished. We decided to have a fiddler's contest and sev-eral other novel features, including a greased-pig catching con-test. There is still a question about whether to have a teamster contest and a drawing contest, but we will probably have them. They are good for bringing a crowd, for most people like to watch them.

Monday, July 25. Fair and hot. I tried my hand at salesmanship today — with good success, if I do say so!

I wanted to prove that it could be profitable if it was handled right, especially after having the job thrown at me at the last minute. Bobby and I started out at about ten with the back of the car loaded with peas. We had them all sold before one and had more orders to fill. We came home and picked some more and sold all of those but half a peck. We could have sold them, but the job was new to us and we were both too tired to bother with one little lot. But we have orders for more peas to go Wednesday and Saturday. All those were sold within a radius of ten miles, and we didn't go north of us at all.

Jean tried to keep the home fires burning the best she could. She went with us in the late afternoon, but she got most of the three meals today. She still needs direction for a big meal like dinner, with so many details to confuse her.

We sold beets, carrots, and cabbages, too, to the summer people. Most of the natives have their own gardens.

Wednesday, July 27. Sunny and hot in morning, cloudy in afternoon. Yesterday Thelma Martin called and invited us to go swimming. Bobby and Rob were picking peas so I went out to the garden to get them. They brought in the peas they had picked, and we put on our bathing suits and went. The water was grand. The beach was sandy where the Martins go swimming, in the West River, near Brookline, and although the water was deep enough for swimming, it was not so deep that the bigger children couldn't touch bottom most of the way across.

Jean said, "This is luxury," and repeated several times, "This is luxury."

She was right. Nothing else we could imagine doing would have been more fun nor have felt so refreshing and good. And what more is luxury?

We tumbled into bed as soon as we got home, relaxed and happy and fell asleep almost at once. But it didn't last long with me. Soon I began to dream about selling peas and it wasn't long before I was wide awake and sleep was impossible. I began to anticipate the ordeal ahead of me when I had to sell them again. I knew it was silly and stupid and all the rest, to dread going to kitchen doors, and asking people if they wanted to buy some peas, but I couldn't help it. Finally, along toward morning, I fell into a deep sleep of exhaustion.

We meet such interesting people in the homes where we

stop, and so far all of them have treated us with delightful courtesy. At one place a tall man strode out of a field at my call. He had long white mustaches and heavy wrinkles around his eyes, but he carried himself like a young Viking and his blue, blue eyes were piercing and sharp. His old straw hat and khaki trousers might have been a uniform, the way he wore them. I could well believe the report that he was one of the most brilliant men in the country. And then the Viking's wife came up and I added to myself, " — but rather hard to live up to."

Mrs. Viking was sweet and she fluttered anxiously. Her straight short black hair was held back from her face by a bandana, twisted carelessly around her head. The upper part of her body was carried slightly forward, as if her hands were forever trying to get places before her hurrying feet could possibly make it. One could see that she was entirely unselfish, and that her one consuming desire was to serve the magnificent male who was her husband.

She bought some peas and ordered more to be delivered Monday, along with some other vegetables. "Are they fresh?" she asked me a number of times, and then again, "Are they fresh, yes?" She talked with a strong Swedish accent. I assured her honestly that they were. "But *please* come in the morning," she begged, earnestly. "My husband likes to rest in the afternoons and does not like to be disturbed. I had rather you did not come at all than to come in the afternoon, yes?"

"Yes," I told her.

In the late afternoon, Bobby and I went into the garden and picked more peas. A thundershower was coming up, and the men had hay out which they were trying to get in before the rain wet it again.

And there, among the peas, I saw a most remarkable display of nature's fireworks. Huge thunderheads were formed in the northwest and a hard wind drove them toward us. Lightning flashed in huge zig-zags straight down to earth. The majestic battle in the sky thrilled me and I wanted only to watch the storm and feel it. The wind rose to a gale. The summer squash vines were bent by the wind until all the stalks touched the ground to get away from the force of the storm. My hat blew off and I let it go, loving the feeling as the wind tore at my hair. It felt like a cool wave on my bare back and legs. I was part of the storm, and I hurried to fill my basket before the rain fell. I could see sheets of rain falling in the distance, through slits in the mountains.

But the rain held off. I looked at the sullen, angry clouds and thought they must spill over immediately, but they passed over my head and others came. Lightning cut ragged holes through them and I could see spots of white clouds high above the thunderheads, and still only a few scattered raindrops fell. Then, all at once I realized that the black clouds had all passed overhead like a routed army scurrying to cover after a defeat in battle, and they had not stopped even to drop one bomb.

Friday, July 29. Occasional thundershowers all day. There must have been a succession of thundershowers all last night. I roused several times during the night, hearing the thunder roll and the rain falling. But the thunder was far away until early this morning when a shower hit nearby and the rain fell in torrents. There were washouts on many roads around, although our road was not much affected.

The children have been asked to sing at an entertainment in Newfane a week from tonight. Both Bobby and Jean had planned to do it, but Jean has been chosen as a delegate from her 4H club to go to Camp Waubanong next week, beginning Tuesday. If she goes to camp Bobby plans to sing alone. Jean is thrilled at the prospect of going since this would be her first camp experience.

Bobby and Mary Martin both received letters tonight from the president of the Historical Society of Windham County. Both of them are among the prize-winners in the essay contest they entered last month. They are supposed to read their essays at the Court House in Newfane next Wednesday. The positions of the prize-winners will not be made public until the meeting.

Rob wants me to hire help in the house next year and make a business of selling peas. It doesn't look too good to me!

Saturday, July 30. Cloudy, but for a wonder it didn't rain. Bobby and I started out at nine o'clock this morning, with our car full of vegetables. I was out in the garden before six o'clock getting the vegetables ready. The dew was thick in the garden and my shoes and socks were soaked long before I was ready to leave. But everything was beautifully fresh.

After the vegetables were gone we went to Brattleboro to do some intensive shopping. This is a good time of the year to find bargains if one knows just what the family needs and is likely to need during the coming months, and is not lured too strongly by the price tags.

We bought Jean some sun suits, a pair of sneakers, some stockings and some flashlight batteries for the flashlight she plans to take to camp. She was thrilled with everything. The clothes fitted perfectly except the top part of one sun suit. I set over the buttons on that and it was all right. Mr. Buchanan, the County club leader came up tonight and okayed her 4H report, so everything is arranged but the money, and Jean's leader assured her that would be ready. The club pays half her expenses.

Sunday, July 31. Warm, and fair all day. Rob felt quite ill today so I stayed home from church to be with him. I'm afraid it's his appendix again. I wish he could be persuaded to have it taken out while there is time, but he feels that every season of the year is the hardest time of year to leave his work. It *would* be hard to pick any special time as convenient for illness.

AUGUST

TUESDAY, *August 2. Fair and warm.* I awoke in the middle of the night thinking about Rob and the terrible chances he is taking with his side. I was sick with worry and tossed and rolled. I thought I was being quiet but Rob woke up and wanted to know what was the matter. I tried to evade his questions but he was persistent and finally I told him.

"I shouldn't worry," he advised me.

But who could help worrying? After he dropped off to sleep I got up and took a blanket downstairs. There I lay down on the couch in the library where I could be miserable without disturbing anyone. I read until dawn — or tried to read — and then I got dressed and started the washing. It was all done by seven-thirty.

The clothes dried fast and Jean's ironing was all done by noon, ready to pack in her suitcase. She was terribly excited and happy about going to camp and Bobby felt glum and cross because he wasn't going. He went last year, so it was Jean's turn this year. I took her to Camp Waubanong this afternoon. June and Bobby went with us as far as Scott Bridge. They went swimming while I took Jean on to camp.

Rob felt miserable this morning and he was all doubled over with pain. He was persuaded to see the doctor, who advised him strongly to go to the hospital now and not wait until haying is done and the crops harvested. Rob's father told him to go now. It looks as if things are beginning to move at last. It is a great relief to know that he will be looked after before it is too late, while there is a good chance that everything will be all right. I don't see how I could bear it if anything happened to him.

Later: Rob is really going. He thinks he cannot get around to go before Thursday because he has to make plans for the work to go on while he is gone, and he has to sell some cows. He told the doctor to telephone the hospital for reservations. I am glad . . . so *glad*. If that old appendix will only wait another day.

Rob isn't a bit perturbed about the operation, but he expects the whole farm will go to pot while he is gone. I told him it wouldn't fail in two weeks so much as if he were gone forever. Of course, there is the expense, too, but I told him it would be a small part of a funeral bill. I have hated to put my worries into words for fear they might really happen, but I am beyond all that now. A spade will be called a spade, and no detours taken.

Wednesday, August 3. Fair and scorching hot. We have all been awfully busy all day today. Today was the day that Bobby and Mary Martin were to read their prize essays at Newfane at the Windham County Historical Society meeting. I didn't have the time to go, but I couldn't deprive Bobby of his chance. And if he had to read his essay about the six generations of Folletts who have lived in this house, with the part about his father, I thought he might choke over it unless I were there to sustain him with my presence . . . although he doesn't act much worried, and we are careful to treat hospital experiences as just another job to be done and no hysterics needed.

I needn't have worried. Mary Martin got first prize and Bobby second prize in their groups, and only the two first prize winners in the two groups had to read their essays. Mary certainly deserved the first prize and we are all glad she got it. She worked long hours over it.

Aunt Florence Follett is going to stay here and look after things while I go to the hospital in Burlington with Rob. That relieves my mind of the folks at home. They will be well looked after if she is here. John, Rob's brother, is going to take us to Burlington tomorrow in his new roadster. It will be much more comfortable than riding in our old car.

Rob took Father's truck and went to Bellows Falls this afternoon after a man to help John with the work. He is an old man by the name of Mr. Yates. Rob thought that he might putter around and accomplish about as much as a younger man, and he was the only man we could find at once who needed a job. He was here when we got back from Newfane.

I baked beans and pies and cake this morning to leave for the men, but I didn't get time to get the ironing done. So tonight after supper, I ironed all the things we will need while we are gone. It was late when I got through and I am dreadfully tired. But still I am held up by a queer sort of buoyancy. I'll probably go on in this way until after the operation, possibly longer, until all danger is past, which please God, won't be long. It's easier, in a way, now we are doing something about it, than it has been for so long, fretting against Rob's unwillingness.

We are to start for Burlington early in the morning so we can get there before noon. Rob is already in bed and sleeping like a baby. He has absolutely no personal fear, and never has had, but if one of the rest of us was going he would be terribly nervous.

I am reminded of all the times when Rob has done dangerous things, absolutely fearlessly. The time he climbed the flagpole to put up new rope when no one else would do it; the bull he used to ride in from the pasture with only a small stick to

guide the beast; the way he will walk the ridgepole of a building, upright, and his hands full. . . .

He is a thoroughbred. He will come through all right, I know,
if we can only get there in time.

Friday, August 5. 10:50 A.M. I am sitting in the waiting room at
the hospital, waiting for Rob to come out of the operating
room. Sharing the room with me are two men and a small boy
of about nine years. The men talk freely. Their wives are being
operated upon. But the boy can't talk. He is having a hard time
trying to be a man. If he opens his mouth to reply to a question,
he has to wipe away tears with his coat sleeve, and he hates
that.

The army man, whose wife is in an operating room, said,
"You hear of operations and accidents, or read about them, and
they are just another thing. But when it is someone you love
who is involved . . . then it is another story."

This waiting is hell. But the little boy troubles me. I wish I
could do something to help him. He is so alone, waiting, with
his eyes glued to the door. Someone said he came with a man
— possibly his father — early this morning. . . .

And then, searching for something to interest the boy, I saw
a stereopticon slide, with a box of pictures, on the big table
beside me. "Have you seen these?" I asked the boy.

He nodded.

"I haven't," I told him. "Would you be willing to show me
how it works?" Gallantly, he walked to my side, and seriously
helped me adjust the slide. We looked at the pictures together,
showing each other interesting details of the pictures which we
liked. There were many pictures which he hadn't looked at
before.

As we talked carelessly about the pictures, his composure
returned, and he told me that his name was Bobby. When I told
him that my boy's name was Bobby, too, he felt that he really
knew me. He was waiting, with his little satchel, for a "Doctor

Screwtacks," he said. His father had brought him, but had had to leave to go to work. There was a bunch on the back of his neck. . . .

Time went more quickly, and I realized that I might have to leave almost any minute. I couldn't bear to leave the little fellow alone again. A doctor came to the door and I stopped him and told him the little fellow's story. The doctor Bobby was waiting for was Dr. Trueaxe.

Then Rob's nurse came for me. Rob opened his eyes when he heard me coming and said sleepily, "Hello, Mother. Have you a kiss for me?"

He came through his operation very well. He wanted to have me stay with him, but the supervisor wouldn't let me. "Hell, you're pretty strict, aren't you?" Rob drawled. But he didn't remember saying it afterward.

When I visited him in the afternoon and evening he was still too groggy to know what he was saying, but he didn't look too ill, and it's such a relief to have it done, with no ruptured appendix and no complications. Much as I hate to, I'll have to go home Monday.

Townshend, Vermont
August 9, 1938

Dearest Rob:

I will write a little while I am waiting for the men to come in to supper. If John should happen to go downstreet tonight, I want to be able to send this along.

The paper with this letter explains itself, I think. Mr. Cutts wrote the heading. Isn't that the nicest thing to do? Except their help getting in the hay. The story would have been even better only a shower came up about four-thirty and stopped the work:

R.C. Follett
Townshend, Vt.

We the undersigned Friends and Neighbors heartily wish you a speedy recovery and a safe return to your home:

I.E. Bills	Reuel Cutts
Ernest W. Cooley	John H. Greenwood
S.B. Martin	F.O. Lawrence
C.A. Shine	O.E. Lawrence
Bert C. Brown	Royal G. Cutts
Joe M. Perry	O.W. Follett
Ralph W. Newell	F. Stewart
Fritz Tier	Charles Ballentine
Lyle Fletcher	Merrill Hall
Lyman Gale	John Holden
Royal B. Cutts	Gordon Aither
Stanley J. Bills	Bob Burton
V.W. Bugbee	E.H. Stacy
R.A. Lewis	John P. Lewis

Kenneth Cooley

Some of the hay had to be turned twice this morning. At noon there was none raked. But after dinner, until the time it rained, they got in twenty-six loads of hay. Harry Carleton sent his truck up, with Claude Shine driving, and there were several teams: Dickson's, Cutts', Martin's, and, I think, another one or two. For about an hour and a half they were unloading hay from both sides of the barn. Ralph Newell drove his truck on the hay fork rope. John was the only one, he said, who could manage the hay fork, and his hands are raw inside where the rope burned them.

There are only a few scatterings left in the big mowing below the house, hardly a load. Altogether, the men estimate that there are six or seven loads out, which could have come in if the rain had held off another hour. There is some hay yet to cut, but I couldn't find out just how much. Some of them plan to come back tomorrow if it is a good day and finish up.

A few brought their dinner and wouldn't come into the house to eat, but there were twenty-four for dinner and three more came in for ice cream and cookies. We began to wonder if the ice cream would hold out, so we started by giving small dishes. (We only had one gallon freezer full, not having anticipated such a large crowd.) But there was enough left so Jean had a dish full when she got home from camp. Mother and Aunt Mattie and Thelma Martin were here and helped me.

Later: John didn't go down to the village tonight, so you may not get your letter quite so soon. He went right to bed after supper.

Jean had a grand time at camp but she is glad to get home. I think it has done her lots of good. She got her 4-H emblem. She learned to do several different swimming strokes, to swim under water, to float, and a little about diving.

Do you know yet when you can come home? Nothing seems just right without you, and while I am doing my work I often forget what I am trying to do, thinking about you and wondering how you are. Somehow, Mister, you disturb my peace of mind when you are away. It must be I love you.

I got your first letter this morning. Mail comes more quickly here than toward the north. It was grand hearing from you and knowing you are getting better all the time. You won't be able to climb stairs right away, will you? Now you have come so far you don't want to undo everything. I want you to feel the best possible.

Mr. Lohman stopped this afternoon and said to tell you, "Hello," from the old man at Deerbrook. Mrs. Lohman has gone to the city for a while. Four or five of the young campers are coming over Thursday to get their hair cut.

Tomorrow will be another busy day and I must get to bed

and also let you rest your eyes, dear one. I wish you were with me.   MURIEL.

Dearest Rob:

Another day has almost gone on the time you will have to be away.

Mr. Ketcham called up this morning before he went to the Milk Plant meeting, to ask how you are and if there was anything he could do. He said that if he had known about the bee yesterday, he would have come up.

John Follett came over this morning with three Finns. Mr. Wiggins sent them over to help hay. They got in all that was ready, helping our folks a lot. Mr. Bills and Mike also came up, and Bobby Burton was over again. I wrote Mr. Wiggins a note of appreciation, and tried to express my gratitude to all the men who have helped.

I had understood that all the hay in the big mowing was cut, but John says that piece where you planted corn last year, away over in the corner, is left standing, and some hand mowing around the road, etc. A little more of that heavy hay at the Woods' place wasn't ready to come in this afternoon. Our gang can finish easily in two or three more days of good weather. Father says that Mr. Yates is improving. He thinks that he wasn't used to this kind of work when he came.

We had some change in weather last night. The thermometer was down to forty-eight this morning at 6:30. I had to put an extra blanket on my bed during the night, and I wished I had you to cuddle against. The day has been clear and fine. Maybe we will have some good weather for a while.

Mother and I made gallons of ginger drink for the men. John F. said they liked it a lot. When he came in this morning he asked if I had any beer; he said Finns were great on beer. I didn't, so we fixed the ginger drink as a substitute.

I had another prize package from Miss Dunlap. About the same kind as usual, although from the card she wrote you would think she was giving me something special. Here's part of it:

"The parcel I am sending you today contains some of the best all wool goods ever manufactured. You cannot purchase such now at *any* price." (I wouldn't want to, the color is streaked and there are moth holes.) "I hope there is enough for a jacket or skirt. If so, you will *never* need another. It will last forever! I am also sending a quantity of velvet pieces. If anyone can use them you can." I gave the velvet pieces to Aunt Mattie who thought she could use them in a rug!

You had a letter from Hal Bantorn of Connecticut, this morning, saying that he planned to bottle your syrup and asking for directions and for addresses of label companies. I have written him and will send the letter in the morning.

We had baked beans and vegetable hash for dinner today. Not knowing how many to plan for, we had plenty left, but we will try to have it eaten up before you get home.

I know you must be all right, but you are so far away and I would like so much to see you. I suppose Uncle John will be there tomorrow, and I had a card from Anna this morning, saying that you were coming along well. *Please* be careful and don't try any crazy stunts.

With lots of love,
MURIEL.

Friday, August 19. A fine, clear day. Slightly cooler. Rob is home! This has been a long, hard day, but such a satisfying one!

Our car wasn't in shape to make such a long trip, and would not have been too comfortable. Anna Ela offered last night to lend her Oldsmobile roadster. I hesitated to borrow any one else's car, but she was so kind about it, and it would be the best thing for Rob, so I finally accepted her offer with gratitude.

I was so excited that I couldn't sleep much last night. I kept waking up and turning on the light to see what time it was. Finally, at half past three, I gave up trying to sleep. After all, the more quickly I started, the sooner I would see him, and there were 125 miles to go, each way.

I got breakfast for the family before I left, all but making the toast. At 4:45 A.M. I was on my way. The Oldsmobile worked beautifully. I handled it cautiously until I became accustomed to the quickness with which it responded to my touch — much faster than our older Buick. Then, too, the world was still dark, and there were unexpected stretches of road which were fog-filled.

I drove up to the hospital at exactly eight in the morning. Rob heard me open the screen door on the porch outside his room and said he knew it was I. He was watching the door as I came in. He was lying on the outside of the bed, dressed in slacks over his Johnnie. He slid off the bed and came to meet me before I could stop him.

He wasn't expecting me so early and wasn't ready to go; he had to have a fresh dressing put on before he left. But we were ready to start back by nine. We stopped at his uncle's house to tell them that we were on our way home, and then got going. We were back in Townshend at five minutes of one. I drove more slowly coming back so I wouldn't jar Rob or make him sway as we went around the many turns and curves. He didn't feel very tired when he got home, and the ride didn't bother him half so much as I expected. I began to get sleepy along the last part of the trip, for 250 miles is a nice little jaunt to take before dinner in the middle of the day.

Mother came up home and got dinner for the gang. I don't know what I would do without her help.

We had lots of callers during the afternoon and evening. I thought Rob would be exhausted, but he wasn't. He must be unusually strong and tough to come through so well in so short a time.

I had the north room, which we have used as a study and

library, made into a bedroom so Rob wouldn't have to climb stairs. It is a pleasant room, with its hand-carved woodwork and beautiful view from any of the four windows. It will be a nice place to receive callers — if he stays in bed long enough.

I went to a Fair meeting at the village at night.

Saturday, August 20. Partly cloudy. Not much change in temperature. Rob apparently feels fine and hates to stay put in any one spot. He even went down into the garden this afternoon and pulled a few weeds. He said it rested him. What a man! He insists that he is being careful and will do nothing to strain his incisions. He walks around with a cane, sort of bent over, and says he still has a kink in his middle, but he knows it won't hurt him to exercise a little. He meandered to the upper potato field to see how it was coming, and was much pleased at the way the plants looked.

The men sprayed the potatoes this morning, and got in a load of hay over at the Needham's. This afternoon, they went over to the horse farm and helped Royal get in oats. They didn't get home until 7:30 P.M. and all of them were about exhausted from the oat dust and chaff. They looked like black men, covered all over with sweat and dust. Bobby did all the chores, even milking ten cows. He was so pleased with himself that he walked over to the Horse Farm to tell the men about it. He drove the horses home on the lumber wagon and unhitched and fed them. He couldn't quite get the heavy harnesses off.

Monday, August 22. Rainy. Tomorrow is our Fair Day. I hope it is a pleasant one. All day we had been busy getting things ready. Jean is to be a Japanese girl in the children's parade, mostly because she already has a Japanese kimono. I have been fixing a black wig for her to wear and she has some grease paint of the proper shade for the part. Bobby isn't going to enter. He thinks he is too old for a children's parade. They both plan to enter the sports events, however.

I have never done so little getting ready for the Big Day before, since the Fair was started four years ago to raise money for the children's health work. It couldn't be helped this year.

Tuesday, August 23. Perfect weather — bright and fair but not too hot.
Townshend Fair is over for the fourth consecutive year, and it was a success. The day was perfect; there must have been two thousand people there. The morning events went off well; the children's sports, the wood-chopping contest, horseshoe pitching, sheep dog demonstration, the children's parade, the horse-drawing contest and the horse jumping exhibition.

Jean got first prize in her class in the children's parade — a pretty flowered voile dress — but neither of my children placed in the sports events.

The horse-drawing contest took longer than had been planned because there were so many entrants. Many were enthusiastic about it and could have watched it all day. The ball game between the Townshend Ramblers and the team from Wardsboro was a fast one with a score of 10 to 3 in favor of the Ramblers. The sheep dog demonstration and coon dog trials were of considerable interest. Many people came from long distances to see them.

After a speech by Representative Charles Plumley on the American flag, and a talk by Judge Preston Gibson of Brattleboro on child welfare and juvenile delinquency, Governor Aiken spoke from an improvised platform on the fair grounds. He spoke on the flood control issue. He reminded us that we were gathered on one of the very spots the federal government proposes to seize from the state of Vermont as a site for a flood control dam. "The federal government is after the very ground you are standing on," he said. "They want the West River valley to play with, but they won't get it."

Governor Aiken traced the history of the controversy through the past two years. He said that harmony existed among the four states involved and that they were well on the

142

way to settling the problem themselves when blocked by the federal administration.

"Last spring," he said, "the President was approached by a committee representing four states, but he held out for federal title to dam sites and power rights not only on the Connecticut but on all its tributaries and all the land draining into these tributaries. This meant federal right to seize most of New England."

Al Marsh, our local butcher, had charge of the fair dinner at noon. It was served in the town hall and was very successful. At night there was an old-time fiddler's contest followed by a play put on by the local Grange, and a dance followed the play. The fiddler's contest drew a crowd, and they were good. Rob attended the fair all day but didn't go at night. He got tired but not overtired, I think.

The day must have been a financial success, too, although we can't tell much about that until all the bills are in.

The exhibits were good; fancy work, flowers, art, photography, 4H Clubs, and so on.

Thursday, August 25. Uncle Abel and Aunt Grace Grout called this afternoon. They live in a charming log cabin on the top of Newfane Hill. He has some botany students, mostly college professors, and he has his own summer school right at his summer home. A nice plan, to have interesting people come to him, instead of his going to them.

Friday, August 26. I had a letter from Judy Clark. She wants to come up over Labor Day week-end and bring her fiancé, whose first name is Bob. Of course I shall write back at once and tell her to come. I don't know just where I shall have her sleep. She had infantile paralysis several years ago, and although she manages to walk quite well again, after two years in bed and several more years with braces and crutches, she cannot climb stairs without a great deal of difficulty. With one downstairs room already occupied by Rob, I wonder whether to put a cot in the living room or dining room for her, or to have Bob carry her upstairs. The latter plan would be the easiest for me.

Saturday, August 27. Cloudy, rising temperature. John went over to the Horse Farm and helped get in oats, Friday. Today the men were over at Needham's getting in hay. This has been the worst year to hay I ever saw. There has been so much wet weather that hay wouldn't dry. We are usually all through long before this, and there are so many other things needing attention. Usually, the men spend at least one day picking berries for me to can. It looks as though I would have to do most of it myself this year, although I don't have much time to go very far between getting meals. I am so tired of getting those everlasting meals. A cake or a batch of cookies are all gone at one sitting. I never saw such appetites.

Monday, August 29. Fair and cool. This morning I did the washing, and in the afternoon Rob and I went down to the village. I had to see the Mannys, who live in a shack below the village. Two of their children need their tonsils out, and the last tonsil clinic comes tomorrow morning at the Brattleboro hospital. Mrs. Manny was anxious to have the boys' tonsils out and would try to pay a little something back to the Health Council when she could. She couldn't promise, she said.

The Mannys and their five little children manage somehow in the little shack of two or three rooms. She entertained me on the rickety porch, only half roofed, so I could only see the inside of the shack through a cluttered open door. She was paring ripe yellow cucumbers, preparing them for pickles. She was almost as dirty as the children, but she had a fine, cordial smile.

When part of the mill burned down, Mr. M. lost his job there. For two weeks, she said, the two oldest boys, six and eight (but in size only four and six), had earned money taking orders for toilet goods and condiments from a mail order house, enough to feed the family. I knew they had trudged for miles, over all the back roads as well as through the village, with a heavy sample case to carry. My neighbors who live nearer the village had told me about the little boys coming. I live far enough away so they didn't get here. The mill owner does all he can for them, and gives them the use of the shack rent-free, until the mill is built up enough so that Mr. Manny can be employed again. Now Mr. M. has a few weeks' work on the road.

The last two children were born without benefit of a doctor. He wasn't even called. The nearest neighbors didn't know about the advent of the last one until the baby was two or three days old, then the mother let the children tell about it at school. The woman who lived upstairs in the same house said she was sure she had heard Mrs. M. walking around downstairs each day.

When hot lunches are served at school the children fill up with all they can hold. The mother sent word to the teachers that they were to get only one helping, but they always have all they can eat, which is usually at least three helpings. The mother is very proud, and they try to keep off the town. They are the kind of people who ought to be helped to help themselves, I believe.

I stopped at the Doctor's and he plans to take the children to the hospital with him when he goes in the morning. I hope they will grow a little now.

The Lohmans called this evening. They said their place had been sold. They felt sad about it. They have felt that Vermont has been a cure-all for all their ailments, and they want to buy a smaller place somewhere in this section. Mr. Lohman has improved greatly in health during his stay this summer. Mrs. Lohman is a dear. I hate to lose her for a neighbor.

Wednesday, August 31. Very foggy all day. Light mist at times. Jean and I spent most of the morning making sweet cucumber pickles. Jean is keen about canning and is anxious to do all she can of it. We had seventeen cans of pickles, about evenly divided between quarts and pints. They will taste good next winter.

Rob pared a big pan of apples and I made two deep-dish apple pies and some apple sauce. We had one apple pie for dinner. We could have eaten both pies if I hadn't hidden one for another meal. All the family went for it in a big way.

John went over to Father's hill farm this morning to spray potatoes with the power sprayer, while Everett has been drawing water with Father's truck this afternoon to fill the sprayer for our potatoes. The water is drawn into a big tub from which it is piped directly into the sprayer, to be mixed with the copper sulphate, commonly called blue vitriol, and dust. Most of our potatoes now have a blue coat of vitriol which covers the leaves. This is bad weather for blighting, or rather, the conditions are all too favorable for it. The tops of Father's potatoes have started to blight in spite of every precaution.

The two Tucker children, Dorothy and Harold Davis, and one of their friends came to see Bobby and Jean this afternoon. The Tuckers were given one of the baby rabbits to take home with them when they were up before. Today they wondered if they could buy another one to go with it. Bobby and Jean let them have one. It was the last one of the baby rabbits because four of them have died. The male rabbit broke into the pen where they were and killed them. The children were heartbroken and they held a funeral for the rabbits and buried them carefully. More are expected soon, or the children wouldn't have been willing to part with the last baby.

SEPTEMBER

S ATURDAY, *September 3. Fair and cool. Brisk wind. Temperature 32° at 6 A.M.* Rob was especially anxious to help me this morning because I had so much to do, getting ready for company and doing my Saturday's baking and everything. So he decided that this was a good day to clean the stove and take down the stove pipe.

"But I can't do my baking while the stove is being cleaned," I protested.

"The stove and pipe are full of ashes," Rob answered, "and I think you would be ahead in the long run if they are clean. Now if you will let the fire go out . . . "

So I refrained from putting more wood into the stove and finally, when the fire was out, he had John take down the stove pipe and empty it outdoors while he cleaned the stove. Now (as anyone knows who has experienced the process) the atmosphere is apt to be blue with words as well as soot before the stove is ready to use again. This morning was no exception. And the kitchen floor was beyond words. It needed two baths before it was presentable. And all this on a Saturday morning when I was trying to bake. I didn't! By the time the fire was going briskly in the clean stove, it was time to get dinner and I was the one who was blue.

Maybe my growing nervousness transmitted itself to the children, for they squabbled more than usual and I spoke sharply to them more than once. If I had had time to stop everything and talk to them, I think they would have quieted down, but they were like spirited horses and rared the more whenever I reprimanded them.

Rob and Bobby went after blackberries this afternoon. I tried to keep Rob from going because of the lifting but he said, "I never saw a blackberry yet that was so heavy it weighed anyone down." He drove the car almost to the blackberry patch and Bobby carried the heavy pail home when it was full. And the blackberries grew high enough so he didn't have to stoop much. They brought home about ten quarts.

Three artist friends of Rob's cousin, Francis Colburn, stopped late this afternoon. They are exhibiting some of their paintings at Manchester, Vermont, this week, as is Francis. Francis was unable to come but he asked his friends to look us up. They are delightful people and one of the men is Francis' art teacher. They stayed here a while and then went over to the Horse Farm to see the horses. When they came back, they set up a target in the field in front of the house and practiced shooting with a twenty-two rifle and a pistol of the same caliber. I presume they can hit a canvas with more accuracy than they hit the target.

Rob and I shot at the target, too. Rob had his thirty-two special brought out, but his hand isn't steady enough yet to drive tacks, as he usually can.

Judy and Bob Abbott were late arriving. Judy is the same dear person she always was, but dreadfully thin — only weighs ninety-eight pounds. Bob Abbott, whom we had never met before, is a fine chap. He has a good position on a Waterbury, Connecticut, daily paper.

Sunday, September 4. Foggy in morning, clearing to beautiful weather in afternoon. We packed a picnic dinner into the automobile today and went to the top of Putney Mountain to eat it. The day was lovely and warm, although we needed sweaters when we sat down and were quiet. We roasted "angels on horseback" on long sticks over a fire and everyone came back for more. They are a delicious concoction made by wrapping a small hunk of cheese in a strip of bacon and toasting them over an open fire. There was a gallon of ice cream to divide among six of us. We weren't able to lick the freezer at one sitting, after all the "angels" we ate.

I forgot to mention that I put up six and a half quarts of blackberries this morning. I couldn't wait until tomorrow to can them because they would have spoiled.

John was late getting back tonight and when he came he brought Frank Earl, whom Rob has hired to help with the fall work. That will make only one more to feed, but it seems like the last straw.

Tuesday, September 6. Cool. Light frost last night. Judy and Bob Abbott left yesterday morning. He had to be back at work this morning, and they wanted to go home by way of the Mohawk Trail.

Although there was a light frost last night, it did no damage on our farm. It cut some of the crops in the valleys, however. I have a lot of canning which must be done before frost strikes. Since I was unable to do more the past month, I must make a great stab at it during the time which is left.

We canned twenty-three cans of corn today. Rob helped me cut it off the cobs and get it ready for the cans. This afternoon I had a three-hour ironing to do. I didn't finish it until after supper.

The stove worked terribly in spite of its cleaning. I made three pies over an hour before dinner, and they weren't done in time. The cinnamon rolls, which I made out of the leftover pie crust, got done, and the men had those for dessert, with a few cookies left over from last night. I was busy with the canners and didn't get time to eat until long after the men had finished. About fifteen minutes before the men came in to dinner, I realized that I had no bread, and that I was unable to get any in time, so I had to make biscuits. No one objected, in fact, they ate them up in short order, but I had to leave the canning for that extra time. The two jobs, cooking and canning, clash somewhat.

The children began school this morning, rather glad to go back again, when the time actually came, although they weren't wild with anticipation beforehand.

I hadn't realized how the children had grown this summer until Jean put on her school dresses. She lived in sun suits all summer, only putting on her good dresses when she went somewhere special, and Bobby has worn shorts and, occasionally, a shirt. Jean's dresses are two inches shorter than they were in the spring. I hope they will do for this fall, until she puts on her thicker dresses. Bobby's school pants are very short for him and will have to be lengthened at once.

Bobby still sleeps outdoors in his tent and he plans now to sleep there all winter, but I imagine he will come into the house when the first snow falls.

Thursday, September 8. We have been canning more today; four cans of broccoli, four of blackberries and one of applesauce.

After the supper dishes were done tonight, I cut out a green bouclé knit suit. I cut it out on the living room floor, where there was plenty of room to stretch out. I am going to Brattleboro Saturday afternoon and want to wear the suit. I have a green felt hat to match, and I'm going to dye my white gloves a natural tan to match the blouse of the suit. It ought to look nice.

There are predictions of a heavy frost tonight. The moon is nearly full and it floods the earth with an exquisite beauty. The air is decidedly spicy, and it smells of all the good things the earth has given us. Ripe corn in the husks and pumpkins and cider apples, and all the other fruits of the soil. The earth itself has a different odor at this time of year, more brash and heavy than in the soft springtime or rich summer. And over everything that enormous, golden harvest moon hangs low.

Friday, September 9. Cool and clear. Light frost last night. The frost did little apparent damage in this section last night but there were heavy frosts along the brooks in the valleys. I can understand why the early settlers chose their homes on the uplands instead of in the valleys where frost usually strikes earlier.

Monday, September 12. Cloudy, with occasional showers. Warmer. Rob has been selling potatoes today. The market price is only fifty-five cents a bushel, which is discouraging, as there is no profit for the farmer who has to sell at that price. Quantities of potatoes are flooding the markets, according to reports, because they are rotting in the fields in several states to the south and west of us. According to available market reports, the estimated potato crop for September falls nearly eight million bushels below that estimated in August. Eventually, that ought to force the price of potatoes higher, if the farmers can afford to hold onto their crops long enough.

My green suit is an awful disappointment. It looked nice and fitted well when I first put it on, but after it was worn for a while it kept stretching and stretching until now it is large enough for two of me. I don't know what to do about it, or whether it will ever stop stretching. And I had planned on wearing that costume a lot this fall. I am going to hang it up in the closet for a while and let it stretch all it will and then maybe it can be cut down again to fit.

Tuesday, September 13. Fair and warm. Cloudy in late afternoon. A beautiful Indian Summer day! I would have liked nothing better than to have spent the day loafing in the woods.

I did the ever-present washing this morning. I was late getting it done because the electricity went off just before I started, and although I did the sheets out by hand so they would be dry in time to put back on the beds before night, I waited for the electricity before I finished.

Today was the primary election, and since Rob was a ballot clerk, he had to be at the town hall by ten this morning. I rushed around and took him down so I could have the car to use. Then I had to hurry home to get dinner ready in time for the men. I am heartily tired of this constant rushing about. I didn't stop to vote this morning.

Monday, September 19. It has rained nearly every day for a week — "Rain, Rain, go away, come again some other day," was one of the verses I used to teach to the first graders when I taught school. I wish there were some way to make it stop now.

The men have been doing some odd jobs around the house, cleaning the cellar, building new potato bins, and cleaning the back kitchen, which is a clearing house for junk and tools and everything one could imagine and many things one would never expect to find anywhere. Sometimes I am inclined to believe that the vaunted New England thrift is only an ingrained aversion to throwing anything away, even junk.

I have seen Father, off on a vacation, find a discarded piece of scrap iron, and put it in the car and carry it home several hundred miles because it "might come in handy some time."

There is still some fall cleaning that I would be glad to have the hired men do, but Rob thinks they might feel insulted if they had to get down on their knees and scrub.

Tuesday, September 20. Still it rains, sometimes gently and sometimes in torrents. News comes over the radio that the storm is assuming the proportions of a flood. A bridge has gone out in East-hampton, Massachusetts, but Connecticut is getting the brunt of the high waters. Two dams have already gone out.

Also, we have kept the radio going steadily for days, listening to news of the European crisis. England and France expect Czechoslovakia to give up the Sudeten territory, and Poland says that if Germany gets her slice, Poland ought to get back her part of Czechoslovakia. Rob says he hopes the Czechs will stand firm, but I wonder what they can do, with the big European powers backing down on their promises. It is a shame.

The two hired men, John and Early, are taking a vacation today. There is not much they can do around here while the rain continues. That helps me out a lot; the amount of necessary cooking has decreased amazingly.

Wednesday, September 21. Hard rain. Early this morning we heard over the radio that Czechoslovakia has conceded to England's and France's demands and agreed to surrender the German Sudeten area; also, that Hitler has assembled a large army at the German border, where they are ready for anything Hitler might order. Hitler has agreed to respect the rights of the rest of Czechoslovakia. I wonder if he will respect anything, or if this is only a scheme to gain an entrance into the country.

The Whitneys called us on the telephone this morning and asked Rob what he wanted to do about the ensilage cutter of ours they had hired to fill their silo. They live down in the valley near the West River. The river is still within its banks, but has nearly reached the top, and the Whitneys are afraid their farm may be flooded if the rain continues to beat down as hard as it does at present.

Rob went down to help them move the cutter over across the railroad tracks onto higher ground.

The children came home at noon. The weather bureau predicts a hurricane, and the rain is increasing in force. The roads may be washed out too badly for traffic by the time school is usually out. I was glad the officials dismissed school early. All of us are uneasy, although I don't know why we should be. Bobby still wants to sleep in his tent tonight, but I won't let him if there is danger of a hard wind storm, although the hills protect us here to a great extent.

Thursday, September 22. Fair and beautiful overhead. Chaos underfoot. The hurricane struck last night. I thought that some scenes in the movie, "Hurricane," had been exaggerated. Now I know they weren't. It was thrilling and awful and moving. It brought havoc and destruction and death.

At dusk, the men were outdoors trying to save the roads from being completely washed away. I watched them from a window inside the house as they fought against the wind and the rain. The rush of the wind through the trees was like heavy thunder. The trees writhed and twisted in the wind like live things being tortured. I was afraid that some would fall and crush the men as they toiled, bent to the gale. It made me think of the pounding of the waves against the sea coast, and I was thankful that my men had solid earth under them.

The silo toppled over like so much kindling wood. Bobby's tent fell, leaving his cot exposed to the storm. Slate was torn from the roof of the house. The shed across the road, in front of the house, went down. That was the one happy thing that happened. I had been trying to get it torn down for years. One of the giant Lombardy poplar trees crashed through the telephone wires on Popl' Tree Hill. (The next morning we found that the tree trunk was hollow and that a swarm of bees was occupying it. We must dig them out and see if they have honey stored.)

The lights went out and the telephone went dead. We were isolated from the world. The men barely managed to fight their way back to the house. Jean prowled about from room to room like a nervous cat. Royal blew in, tried to telephone back to his house, and blew out again, hoping he could get his car through

before the road went out. A window crashed in the kitchen over the sink, letting in swirling eddies of water and wind. We lit our one oil lamp and one lantern against the darkness and storm, and thanked the Lord that the men who built this house had built well, on a firm foundation.

The storm cleared in the night.

"We will have more rain in a few days," Rob predicted, "We always do when a storm clears in the night."

This morning we awoke to a shining sun and a sparkling sky, revealing dreadful wreckage everywhere we looked. After breakfast we left everything and went exploring. The farther we went the worse things looked. We were comparatively fortunate, we found.

Father had arrived at our house at dawn, and told us that the bridge leading onto the main road at Simpsonville was partly gone, and the road from our house was mostly washed away, worse than in the flood of '27 or '36. So the milk couldn't get to Brattleboro.

We started down the Peaked Mountain road, by the Morgan Horse Farm. There we were joined by Royal and Caroline and Tommy, the man who works for them. Anna and Janet came along later on horseback. Trees were across the road and there were a few deep gullies in the road, but nothing too bad. But at the foot of the hill the bridge was gone. We thought we would have to go through the woods and across fields to the Harmonyville bridge, to get into Townshend village. Then we saw a big tree in the brook with its roots lodged against some boulders in the middle of the swollen stream and its branches solidly against the opposite bank, about fifteen feet above the water.

"Now if we could find a plank to reach from the shore here to the tree roots," Rob said, "we might climb up the tree to the other side."

We soon found the plank and Royal and Tommy flopped the farther end of it out into the brook against the roots. Tommy walked the plank over the swirling water and made the foundation safe with rocks. Then Rob followed, and they started up the tree. But one small brittle branch held the main branch of the tree away from the farther bank. We called across to a man who lived nearby. He came out with an axe, a crowbar and a shovel and hacked the offending branch away.

Bobby was the second one to cross. Rob stayed halfway up the tree to help Jean over. Jean got halfway between Rob and the farther bank when she happened to glance down. The madly tumbling water fifteen feet below unnerved her, and the limb wasn't any too big around for safety. She couldn't go farther and she didn't dare turn around and come back. She clung there trembling. I stood at the base of the tree, leaning against it, watching, and I could feel the tremor of the tree, she shook so hard. The man who lived on the farther bank went away and soon came back with a clothesline. He threw one end of it to Rob and he and Tommy held the other end firm and Jean clutched that while she walked to safety.

It wasn't the most fun in the world, I decided, to shinny up the trunk of the tree and then walk up the twig-clogged branch over the dirty, boiling water, with only the clothesline to cling to. We all crossed safely, but none of us wanted to go back that way when we went home.

The village was completely isolated. Telephone lines were down everywhere in tangles of trees and wires. Electric light wires were just as bad. Bridges were gone or roads were washed completely away. Anna had a battery radio, and that was the only way we could get word from the outside world.

We walked down to Harmonyville. The bridge still stood, but the approach on the farther side was completely washed away. Hazel Upton barely escaped with her life last night when she and the neighbors took her babies to safety on the other side of the bridge. The approach crumbled away as she stepped on it. She went in to her hip, but the dirt under her other foot held until she stepped on the bridge. Her babies were just ahead of her, being carried by neighbors. The woman walking in back of

Hazel was pulled back just in time. Hazel said she didn't realize what had happened until it was all over; she thought she had merely slipped. But when she turned and looked back . . .

The Truesdales, who live beside the brook, suffered a big loss when all their hens and chickens and laying pullets went down the drink, along with the houses and equipment and a lot of their land. But their ducks came swimming in to breakfast, "as cute as you please," Mrs. Truesdale said.

All the able-bodied men are working like mad getting a road passable to the outside, and fixing bridges. Most of the bridges need some repair, some are completely gone, others are weakened or the road nearby has gone.

The old-timers recall the flood of 1869 when every bridge in town was washed away.

We walked home up the hill from Harmonyville, back of Peaked Mountain. After dinner, still curious, all of us walked down to Simpsonville. We were getting tired and we had already walked more than we had for a long time, but it was the only way we could get places.

It made us feel sick to see the chaos and ruin. Rob is afraid the road won't be fixed this fall, although we will have to get the milk out some way.

The bridge over the brook next to the main road is hanging by one abutment on one side, and only a loose rock on the other side. Nevertheless, we risked our necks and crossed onto the main road. The stone bridge in Simpsonville, which Rob's grandfather built, is still standing staunch and strong. Mr. Knapp said he could remember when that bridge was built. Grandfather put in mud sills of hemlock logs, hewed on one side, and placed them deep under the water. Hemlock never rots under water, and it gave Grandfather something solid to build to, but something which might "give" just enough to avoid having its load break.

The brook had slipped over the road below the bridge and played hide-and-seek all over the neighbors' lawns. We went in to Mrs. Prentiss'. She was feeding a number of stranded refugees. She was still laughing and joking in spite of the extra strain and work, and she is no longer young.

"Well, anyway," she laughed, "We have plenty of nice water."

We walked more than ten miles today. Not such a long jaunt over good roads, but this was mostly over loose boulders and stones and slippery earth.

We have lots of good milk and nothing to do with it.

Friday, September 23. Cloudy, damp atmosphere. Reports are beginning to trickle through from the outside. And the more they come the worse they are. We have *nothing* the matter around *us* compared to the terrible tragedies in our sister towns and states. According to the last reports, more than 250 people in the New England states lost their lives, and houses and land and livestock were washed away.

Today was cloudy and rain threatened, but we had to go on with our usual duties. The children won't have school for the rest of the week, although we hope the roads will be open enough for them to ride part of the way by Monday.

They have been picking cranberries from the bog down the hill beside the road. They picked a number of quarts. This afternoon they gathered butternuts. There are lots of nuts this year — five bushels of butternuts under one tree.

Rob and Mr. Yates worked all day repairing roads with the men at the Morgan Horse Farm. Rob ought not to attempt such hard work, if he does any at all, but he says he is careful and takes all the strain of lifting on his back. There is no stopping him, anyway, although he says a good many people have tried.

They thought at first that the best way, and quickest, to get cars and teams out onto the main road, would be to fix the road down Peaked Mountain until they got nearly to the washed-out bridge, and then turn to the south and follow an old abandoned road down to the Harmonyville bridge, which has been repaired. The milk could be picked up there. But the road men started repairing the road from Harmonyville, up to Martins', back of Peaked, so our men started fixing the latter road from the Four Corners. Our road is passable to there. That road is mostly steep, with difficult pitches, but it will be a way to get out. They hope to have it passable by tomorrow night.

Stan Martin walked in at eight tonight. He is a selectman and he had been walking all over town, trying to estimate the damages and giving orders about what has to be done. He was about exhausted. I don't suppose he had walked so far before in years and years. We gave him a couple glasses of milk and some cake and tried to make him rest longer, but he was anxious to get home.

I did part of the washing by hand today. We may not have power again for two weeks. The wires are twisted and broken into hundreds of fantastic shapes. Many are buried under trees and debris.

Saturday, September 24. Cloudy, with occasional light showers. The men have been away all day working on the road, only coming home for dinner. They got the road through tonight. Rob was all out of milk cans and we have been doubling up for the past two days, putting milk into almost anything we could find, so we took the car down over the rocky, bumpy road to town just before dark and got the empty cans.

It was better going down than coming back up, although our car is heavy enough so it stuck to the road, and high enough to clear the stones and waterbars. Lighter, lower cars don't fare so well.

The children walked to the village this afternoon, down the Peaked Mountain road. They thought it would be fun, and we needed to get a few groceries at the store. We would have waited to get the groceries until we went down at night if we had known the road would be opened by then. They had a five-mile jaunt, but they didn't mind it at all, they said.

Sunday, September 25. Sunny and cool. A beautiful day. The men are now working hard trying to get the road open from here to the main road in Simpsonville, two and a half miles above Townshend Village, but in the town of Townshend. That is our best way of getting out and it is only a mile from here to the main road. But such a long mile. . . .

Monday, September 26. A beautiful day, forerunner of October's bright blue weather. The leaves have begun to take on their fall coloring, although they are not so bright yet this year as usual. They are colored in soft, subdued tones instead of the usual flamboyant colors. I love to be outdoors every possible moment, the world is so lovely, and the days are never long enough for all there is to be done.

And now, with no lights worth mentioning after darkness falls, the days seem much shorter. Dawn comes at about six in the morning — or at least it is light enough to see by that time — and the lamp has to be lighted at six o'clock in the afternoon. We could get more lamps ready to use but we have thought each day that the electricity would be turned on before the following evening, so we have waited another day — and then another.

After the work is done at night and supper is eaten, all the family gathers close around the table where our one and only lamp is, trying to see a few words in the paper, or to mend, or study. Usually we stay in the kitchen after the dining room table is cleared from supper, because I have to finish the work there, and they all get comfortably settled before I get through. And then why should they bother to move? The kitchen is usually the warmest room in the house at this season of the year, and there is quite a chill in the air after the sun goes down.

Tuesday, September 27. Clear in early morning, cloudy and showers all the rest of the day. The Martins and I left for Brattleboro about nine o'clock this morning. A slight thundershower made us wait a few minutes until it had passed. The roads are terrible! We managed to get through to Brattleboro on the river road, although it hasn't been open to traffic long. Much of the road has been washed away by the brooks and the West River, or blocked by trees. Large gangs of men are working in many places on the road, filling in holes and cutting up trees.

It is tragic the way so many magnificent trees which had taken generations to grow were uprooted and broken in a few short hours, but it's remarkable that so many of the trees fell in directions where they did the least possible damage. Trees on lawns often fell in narrow spaces between houses, or on buildings in a way which did little damage. Of course, all the fallen trees were not so accommodating but the miracle was that so many were — or the wind, or the "powers that be."

In many places in different sections of the county, entire buildings were moved or destroyed, but we saw none of that on our way to Brattleboro although many bridges were out along the way.

Wednesday, September 28. Clear, warm. Brisk breeze. This is one of those days when I am thankful that I live in just this particular neck of the universe. Just being alive and out of doors is almost enough joy on a day like this. The air is heady and the sun a blessing, and the beauty of the woods makes one want to reach out one's arms wide to encompass it all.

A strange, restless feeling always comes with the change in the seasons, especially in fall and spring. The air is too energizing; it makes people want to do the impossible, and lots of it. It exhausts people with its potency.

Rob and Mr. Yates have been filling Bert Brown's silo all day. They hoped to finish it today, but they couldn't get set up early enough. The rain yesterday afternoon hindered them half a day. Rob came home exhausted. He did too much. He tried to feed the cutter, and did, for half a day, but the vibration "got him," as he said, and hurt him more than working on the road.

I wish he would not try to do such things until he is stronger.

I went down to Mother's this morning and spent the day with her. I took the ironing and did it down there with her electric flatiron, for she has electricity. We had a nice day. She has a wide porch on the south side of the house, and I plugged in the flatiron cord at the porch light and ironed there. So we were out of doors all day, looking across at the radiant hills and enjoying all the beauties of nature while we were doing the necessary work. The perfect combination, if we must work.

Both children came home from school all bunged up. Bobby had carelessly stuck a pencil lead into the soft flesh in the palm of his hand near his thumb and that was sore. Some nice little boy had kicked Jean on her heel and she was lame and in pain from that.

The men were late getting home tonight, and were planning on Bobby's help with the chores. At first Bobby thought he would be unable to milk because of his hand.

"Do you suppose you can find a way to milk the cows without too much discomfort?" I asked Bobby, as I bandaged his hand.

"I suppose I can try," Bobby answered, doubtfully.

An hour later he entered the kitchen. "I have milked seven cows," he told me. "You were right. I did find a way."

I had him soak his hand in an Epsom salts solution and the wound looks clean and good. I doubt if infection sets in. We will watch it carefully for a few days.

The children have begun taking their cod liver oil. Last year I thought they might be old enough to get along without it, but it was a poor idea. They had more colds than they ever had before. So many epidemics of colds and grippe sweep through a school that children need to have high resistance to keep from contracting them.

Thursday, September 29. Sunny, but slightly hazy. Light fog in the valleys. The men finished filling Brown's silo this morning and dug potatoes the rest of the day. Two men came to watch the digging while the test plot was being opened up. So far, they can find no appreciable difference in yield from the two kinds of fertilizers Rob is trying. The men were here to dinner.

We are still without electricity and we finally decided that it may be weeks before the line is repaired, so tonight we went down to the hardware store and bought extra lamp chimneys and wicks for old lamps we had in the house. We boiled out the burners and the lamps now make *some* light shine in the dark places.

OCTOBER

SATURDAY, *October 1.* Mother and Father went to Grafton yesterday after a calf. They went to Cambridgeport and then back along the road toward Grafton, approaching the town from the other end. The farmer who had the calf lived across the brook where a bridge had washed away. Father managed to slide down the steep bank, cross the brook on a plank, and clamber up a steeper bank to the road on the other side. Then there was the difficulty of getting the agile calf across. The men hitched a rope around the calf's body, swung him down into the deep gully washed by the brook, and then pulled him up the bank on the opposite side. Mother said she imagined the men were glad he wasn't a cow.

The electricity came on tonight. I was getting supper in the dusk, which was so deep it could almost be cut, for even after the lamps were lit the shadows were thick in the corners of the room. And then the electricity flashed on in the fixture over the stove, almost blinding us for a second with its brilliance. The children gave a great shout of joy. Rob hurried into the living room and turned on the radio in time to hear the football scores. Now, we all appreciate the blessings of electricity more than ever before.

Sunday, October 2. Fair and warmer. I heard Bobby tiptoe downstairs early this morning. I knew by the sound that he wanted no one to hear him. I stayed wide awake in bed until I heard him go up to the barn and knew what he was planning to do. He wanted to surprise his dad by doing most of the chores.

When Rob finally woke up, dismayed at the lateness of the hour, and hustled up to the barn, he found that Bobby had already milked seven of the ten cows and had finished all the rest of the chores.

"It was pretty hard to crawl out of bed at half past five," Bobby admitted later, to me, "but I knew Daddy was tired and I thought he would like that surprise."

Bobby is a thoughtful youngster, and so is his sister. Now he is studying the catalogs for bicycles. His dad thinks he can get one soon. That is his pay for his summer's work. He knows just what kind he wants, has it all picked out and would be satisfied with nothing else. His wishes are reasonable so we want to meet them.

Rob and Bobby went through the west sugar orchard this morning. They counted forty-one giant sugar maples blown down in that one lot. They were some of the best running trees on the farm and were big enough to carry six or seven sap buckets apiece. They found the same conditions in the south sugar lot. The hurricane caused over a thousand dollars worth of damage to our sugar lot alone. Considerable timber blew over, too, but Rob hasn't had time yet to go over all our land — five hundred sixty acres — and estimate the damage.

We were fortunate that our land didn't wash away, as it did in many places. But those trees cannot be replaced in our lifetime.

Tuesday, October 4. Sunny, with a light blue haze over the hills. There is an urgency about these fall days, a feeling of haste in the sharp, pungent morning air, as the days gradually become cooler and cooler. There is so much to do and the time before winter comes is growing short.

Vegetables must all be dug and stored in the cellar — those not already in cans; the buildings must be made tight and windproofed against the blasts of winter storms. Warm clothing must be brought out of summer storage, aired and pressed in readiness for instant use if the day suddenly turns cold. Plans for needed additions to our winter's wardrobe must be made. Farmers' incomes are usually small, and especially when crops fail there is much need for the homemakers' ingenuity and skill.

The weather was so beautiful today I turned my back on my household tasks, took my sewing outdoors and basked in the warm sun while I worked. That is one nice thing about living on a farm; I merely step over my threshold and there I am, right smack in the middle of all outdoors where everything is beautiful. The smell of ripening apples, and acrid odor of drying leaves, the bright songs of the birds and the shrill chatter of squirrels are all so deeply satisfying to the senses that it makes one want to run and shout and do all manner of idiotic things. And spread over all is the blue, low-hanging haze; a dusky blue huddles close above the flame-colored trees, like a thin smoke pall over numerous small fires in the woods.

The children brought home two notes tonight, one from the district nurse asking my help in organizing a baby clinic for the eighteenth or nineteenth of October. The other was from the home demonstration agent for this county asking me to give a report on our Health Council work in Townshend at the Farm Bureau finish-up meeting in Brattleboro next Thursday; also, a brief summary of the County Health Institute held in Newfane last May. I shall try to do both.

When Rob and I went to the Parent-Teachers Association

meeting tonight I started the ball rolling by advertising the baby clinic at the meeting.

Wednesday, October 5. Fair most of the day, cloudy toward night. Jean made a chocolate cake for supper tonight and it fell — flat. We had it for supper just the same. Bobby made a number of derogatory brotherly remarks although he ate several pieces of it. Jean disappeared after supper. I noticed it after a few minutes and called to her. I heard a teary little voice answer from the darkness of the living room and I went in and turned on the light. Jean was nowhere in sight. When I called again she answered from the corner behind the open door. There she was, huddled down into a miserable little heap on the floor, crying heartbrokenly. I knelt down and gathered her into my arms.

"I'm never going to make another cake," she burst out passionately. "Never, never. Everyone made fun of it and Bobby said such awful things about it. I'll *never* make another cake."

We talked it over, Bobby apologized and Jean felt better. I'll have her make another cake soon, before she loses her confidence.

Friday, October 7. Beautiful weather, fair and golden. The beauty of the foliage is at its height now and I have been outdoors almost all day, revelling in the splendor of this beautiful world and soaking up the sunshine. Mornings are cold — the temperature was down to twenty-eight degrees this morning — but the sun warms the earth during the middle of the day until it is comfortable to work out of doors without wraps.

Mother, Aunt Lila and my cousin Gladys came early this morning. They wanted me to spend the day with them at Mother's and go over to Laura's with them this afternoon. My dishes weren't done nor my floors swept, but with a deplorable lack of conscience, I stacked the dishes in the sink, locked the door behind me and forgot all about the work until I got home at night.

When we arrived home tonight we had a welcome surprise waiting for us. The telephone had been repaired and the bells were ringing for the first time in over two weeks. All at once we felt close to the outside world again. Sometimes I wonder if we haven't become too dependent on so-called modern conveniences and if we are enough better off than our ancestors were, to pay for the added expenses of electricity and telephones and automobiles. Be that as it may, I know I am much more contented living on a farm because I know I am nearly as close to doctors and stores and the events of the day as if I lived in the heart of a large city. And I have the great advantage of having good neighbors and loyal friends and the great out-of-doors just over the doorstep.

Saturday, October 8. Fair and warmer. There were two extra men here today helping to dig our potatoes. The potatoes in the lower field are yielding lightly, especially on the lower end of the field where flood waters lay for some time. The land is still sodden and heavy with water and the men work in mud, which clogs the potato digger and makes the work slow and disagreeable.

Mary Martin came over this afternoon and Bobby, Jean and Mary worked on their 4-H reports for the year, which have to be in to the Farm Bureau office very soon. They have to keep records of the work done during the year, the costs and time spent, the profits and losses, and they have to write a short story about their year's club work. All this has to be approved by the local leader and the County 4-H Agent before they are awarded their seals of merit for the year's work. Some boys and girls send in reports which would do justice to any business.

Rob and I were talking today with a friend of ours, Mr. Held. He is extremely pessimistic about the lot of the farmers today.

"Farmers haven't a chance to make a decent living," he asserted. "There isn't an agency that is really working for the farmer today. All those which have been set up are actually working toward subsidizing the farmer.

"Some people won't believe me, but this is the way I feel about it. Now these loans that the Federal Government is giving to farmers are given only to those whose credit is good. If they lost everything in the flood and want to get back onto their feet, they can't borrow the money anywhere. And they are obliged to pay plenty of interest. If they can't pay the loan back within a certain time, through circumstances entirely beyond their control, the Government takes away their farms and the farmer is subsidized.

"The people who have nothing and have no initiative to get ahead," he said, "are paid a good salary by the Government to do nothing, but the poor farmer who has nothing to start with but his ability and desire to work, has no chance to get ahead and nobody will help him until he gives up trying to be independent and falls back upon relief. Thousands of good men are lost that way."

He went on about soil conservation practices. "In my opinion that is the greatest gyp to farmers ever perpetrated. Look at Ben Bell. He gets several thousand dollars each year for not raising as many *acres* of potatoes as formerly, but he actually raises more potatoes because he plants the rows closer together. And some poor cuss, struggling to get ahead, is not helped because he has no way of raising the money to begin the practices which would benefit him if he could follow them.

"I would be dollars better off," he said, "hundreds of dollars better off, if I sold my farm and went to work on the road. I would have less than a third as many taxes to pay, I wouldn't work so hard because I wouldn't have the interest in my work I do now, and the hours would be shorter. I am licked at farming before I start. I am not *allowed* to get a decent living. And yet the world is dependent on the crops the farmers raise." And that man was an ardent Democrat a few years ago.

Tuesday, October 11. Fair and warmer. Days like this make up for all the furies the elements send. The men came in to dinner with their faces — and ears — flushed with sunburn. Strange, how those dark days had bleached their skin. I had put away my shorts and halter for the winter, but I fished them out and wore them again today, and then invented jobs which could be done out in the sunshine. It was the kind of a day which drew one right out into the light and warmed one way through to the marrow. It even sent the cows traipsing all over the place with their tails high and their eyes wild, which wasn't so nice.

Royal and his man Tommy helped Rob dig potatoes today. Maybe we shouldn't have unalloyed joy, but it ought not to be necessary to fall so hard quite so often. The potatoes aren't yielding well at all. The rainy season and the late blight, which destroyed the tops several weeks too soon, cut the yield almost in half. There are enough potatoes, but many of them are too small to be marketable. Discouraging. What do people do when the bottom falls out of their plans and hopes and aspirations? What else is there to do but to keep on keeping on? And always the hope that maybe next year. . . If only farm produce prices were equal in value to those of other commodities we must buy, we could struggle through fairly well.

Wednesday, October 12. Fair and hot. Herbert Waters sent some of his wood engravings today. Rob said he didn't think the sap sled in the picture looked strong enough to hold much sap. I reminded him that if he were carving a picture out of wood, he'd probably leave out a few nuts and bolts too. Really we are both glad to have hand-carved illustrations.

Thursday, October 13. Fair in morning, partly cloudy in afternoon. The children were home today and will be for the rest of the week. There is a state teacher's convention Thursday and Friday. I used to like to go to them, when I was a teacher. For one thing, it is usually the nicest time of the year to travel, and the scenery is gorgeous. And then, they usually have such interesting speakers, one comes home from those meetings all puffed with good intentions and enthusiasms. Maybe that was all part of my extreme youth, but I would like to try it again to find out.

I remember the first convention I ever attended. It was at Rutland, and I had been teaching my first school for a little over a month. I was only seventeen and painfully conscious of my youth, but I was just beginning to feel quite grown-up in the company of my elders. And then an enterprising reporter had to spoil it all and burst my little bubble of maturity.

On the second day of the convention he cornered me on the steps of the hall where the meetings were held. I was scared to death of him, that being my first encounter with the press. He was writing a feature story, he said, about the oldest and youngest teachers there. He had already interviewed the oldest teacher and he thought by my looks that I must be the youngest. Would I please tell him my age and give him the details. I was so mortified I could have cried. It was bad enough to *be* the youngest teacher, but to look the part, and have people know it, was too hard to bear!

Saturday, October 15. Dense fog in morning, clearing into a warm, sunny day. This has been a day when everything went backward. Rob and I had to go away this morning on business. We started even before the breakfast dishes were done. But the youngsters finished those and did all the other housework they could find to do while we were gone.

"Aren't we little angels?" Bobby asked.

"Nearly," I told him.

"Well, you needn't worry," Bobby assured me, "my wings haven't begun to sprout yet."

They do such nice things that sometimes I begin to wonder what I ever did to deserve such darling children, and about that

time they break out with some prank that is so exasperating that I wonder what I can ever do with such fiends.

Anyhow, this afternoon, Bobby and Jean asked to go over to the Browns' and we let them go. There was plenty of work left to be done, especially with guests coming tomorrow, and the very thought of sweeping and dusting and polishing gave me a pain. I don't know whether the feeling is real or imaginary because I am so tired of the routine of work, but it feels bad, whichever it is.

The youngsters came home from the Browns' lugging four huge pumpkins. Through an oversight we had forgotten to plant pumpkins last spring and we missed them, both for pies and for jack-o'-lanterns. So the Browns sent two for pies, and two for jack-o'-lanterns. They had more than they could use and are feeding some to their stock. I'm glad we have such nice neighbors.

Sunday, October 16. Fair and warm. We had a happy surprise this morning when Judy and her uncle Rob Clark drove in from Connecticut. They had started at four-thirty this morning so they would have a long day with us. Judy's new husband, Bob Abbott, works on the paper and couldn't get away, but he was good enough to let Judy come without him. They brought us a big basket of apples and some onions which they had bought on the way.

About an hour later, Francis and Gladys Colburn arrived. We were planning on them, as we had invited them several days earlier. The two groups had never met previously but they "hit it off" well from the start, and we all had a grand time. In the afternoon some of them wanted to climb the mountain back of our house, where there is a marvelous view of ranges in four different states which can be seen on clear days. Finally, everyone went but Judy, Jean and me. Judy wanted to go very much, but of course she couldn't walk there.

Judy never complains about her crutches and is always

174

thankful that she can get about as well as she does, but it is not easy to be struck down by polio in youth, as she was. I often think of those two years she spent in bed, flat on her back, with the doctors believing she would never even sit up again; of her long, bitter, yet gallant fight to put new life into the wasted muscles of her body, and to adjust her young ardency to the limits imposed by her broken body. And the other long years of learning to walk again. But her soul grew greater and she became rich in understanding and patience and thoughtfulness.

At first she sat in the lawn chair, leaning far back and gazing out over the bright hills, while I sat on the ground beside her, and then she slipped down beside me and we sprawled comfortably on the browning grass and the brittle dead leaves. We picked up the small dried tree banners in our hands and crumpled them to powder between our fingers as we gossiped, while Jean played busily near us in her house of leaves. Judy told me of her pretty, simple wedding, of her new home, her nice new in-laws, but mostly about the wonderful man she has married. About his thoughtfulness and consideration about the little things which are so vitally important to a woman. Yes, they are very happy, and I believe their happiness will last and grow with the years, as ours has. They have built carefully and were *sure* before they married.

Rob got a partridge today while he was in the woods.

Monday, October 17. Fair and lovely. Warm. According to weather records this is the warmest October in the weather bureau's history. And it can keep on being so for all I care. The woods are dry and many forest fires are raging in different parts of the country. Such a short time ago we were deluged with water and are still trying desperately to repair its ravages.

The spicy warmth made us feel full of ambition. I did a big washing and ironing today and chased cows for good measure. Cows aren't so stupid as many people think. Today one got in the garden through a bar-way separating the garden field from the mowing where the cows were. I drove her back to the bar-way, wondering how she could have got through. The bars were up and looked solidly in place. She looked around at me inquiringly. On general principles I said, "hey," and told her to go on, not knowing what to expect of her. She looked at the bar-way and then at me, as if wanting to be sure I was looking. Then she nonchalantly lowered her head, advanced, and lifted all the bars on her horns, passed through, and let the bars slide off her horns, down her back, and into place again. It was so unexpected and was done with such ease that I just stood with my mouth open in surprise. Then she walked off and went to feeding quietly as if to tell me that she had had her fun and now she was ready to be good.

Tuesday, October 18. Fair and warm. The Baby Clinic was held this afternoon in Townshend at the Congregational vestry. The district nurse hoped we would have at least thirty babies under school age. We had fifty — or fifty-one. The new doctor who is to take Dr. Noyes' place was there, expecting to be an onlooker for the most part. But there were so many babies and so much to do that he was nearly as busy as the other two doctors.

With only a few exceptions the babies were a fine, healthy-looking group, well nourished and beautiful. Where remedial defects were found, the mothers were intelligently correcting them.

Friday, October 21. Fair in the morning, increasing cloudiness in afternoon. Our cows were given the tuberculin test by a veterinary last Tuesday, and he came to read the tests this morning. They are all clear, as usual. We had the dickens of a time getting the cows and young stock into the barn so the veterinary could read their tests. They must have known that something was up; probably they didn't like the needle which had been stuck into them Tuesday. Anyway, they acted like wild things and galloped all over the farm with all of us chasing them.

Saturday, October 22. Fair and cool. Rob went with a load of potatoes this morning, and this afternoon he went over to Royal's to husk corn. Tonight, when he came home, I went to the door to meet him. He had a mischievous twinkle in his eyes and I wondered what would happen. I knew, from long experience with that certain twinkle, that he was planning something. . . .

He never said a word but pulled two red ears of corn out of his pocket and handed them to me. Now, in the country, when a boy finds a red ear of corn and hands it to a girl it means that he wants to kiss her. I laughed and took the hint.

I finished Jean's wool dress with the bolero this afternoon. To brighten it, I embroidered gay wool lazy-daisy flowers marching up each front of the bolero. Jean was entranced with the effect. She stood in front of the dress with her hands clasped under her chin and danced up and down with delight.

"I am the luckiest girl in the world," she said, "and that is the prettiest dress. Mother, I *love* it."

The extra effort was paid for with interest. Then I realized she had no hat to go with her dress when she wore it for best. I had a shapeless old blue felt that Bobby wore out in the rain the night of the hurricane. It had a deep full crown and was several sizes too big for Jean, but the felt was good. The hat blocks had gone back to the Farm Bureau office, but I tried an old stunt of padding a small pail with towels until it was the desired size and shape. Then I steamed the hat until it was damp and had shrunk to Jean's head size. It was ready then to shape. When the hat was only slightly damp I put it on Jean's head and finished shaping it in the way that was most becoming to her. To trim it, I put a plain blue grosgrain band around the crown, twisted a cord of the wool yarns like those on her dress and put it over the ribbon, with a small wool tassel on the side. The hat was modeled after a Deanna Durbin hat and was very becoming to Jean.

It was fun to watch her delight in her new finery. She paraded up and down with her hat on. She even wore it to supper, "to be sure it was thoroughly dry and wouldn't jam."

Tuesday, October 25. Fair. Steady breeze. Cloudy in late afternoon. Sammy barked hard during the night and I woke Rob, but by that time Sammy had quieted. We discovered the reason today. Sammy found a coon in the corn and wanted help. When none came, he got it himself. The wild animals have been working a lot in the small patch of corn left in the garden.

Rob stretched the coon skin on a board. It was a good one. Usually we eat the meat, which tastes much like chicken, but we didn't dare to use this one for fear it had not been bled properly. But Rob and Bobby were anxious to go coon hunting tonight with the dog, a flashlight and the shotgun. It is great sport, they claim, but I'd rather do my hunting by daylight when I can see where I'm going.

They went out for two hours and had a thrilling time, Bobby said. The night was pitch black. Bobby carried the flashlight while Rob walked ahead with the gun. Rob would stop suddenly to listen, and Bobby would bump into him or the butt of the gun before he noticed. He kept stumbling over small sticks and stones. They heard a fox bark nearby. Then Sammy began barking at the foot of a tree. They hurried over, looked up into the branches and saw small beady eyes peering down at them.

Rob shot. The dim shape back of the eyes remained motionless for several minutes. They wondered if the shot had hit. Then it started to slip slowly, slid off the branch and tumbled to the ground. As it came into the beam of the flashlight Rob grunted in disappointment. It was only a porcupine.

The small flashlight they had is not strong enough for night hunting. We will have to get batteries for the larger one. If we could catch enough fur it would partly make up for the loss of the potato crop.

Wednesday, October 26. Rain last night but clear this morning. Slowly rising temperature. Rob and his father went to Brattleboro with a load of potatoes this morning and I went with them.

The children have been invited to a Hallowe'en party at the Davis's next Monday evening, and they are to go as the characters in "Snow White." All of them want to be dwarfs and they have been working on costumes. Bobby and Jean wanted masks of Happy and Doc. I found some for them in Fishman's in Brattleboro.

Rob went up the pasture to look at our spring this afternoon. He took the shotgun almost as an afterthought, because he didn't expect to have a chance to use it. He saw a fox sitting watching him, quite a distance off. He had only number 7½ shells in his gun and didn't expect they were heavy enough to damage the fox much, but he shot once and hit it. Sammy saw the fox almost at the same instant and was after it a second after the shot was fired. Together they got the fox. It had the scrawniest tail I ever saw — more like a weasel's.

Monday, October 31. Tonight is Hallowe'en. The children rushed off to the party at the Davises' after an early supper, carrying their costumes under their arms ready to put on when they arrived. Rob and I waited at Mother's for them until they were ready to come home.

All the children were a most remarkable sight. They bulged with pillows in strange and unusual places. Jean represented the dwarf Doc, and wore a pair of size thirty-eight knickers. Her pillows, stuck in fore and aft, kept sliding down until most of her fatness came around her knees. She was a grotesque little figure with her bearded mask and when she walked she gave a couple of extra twists to the gait of Doc of the movies. We laughed until the tears rolled down our cheeks.

Bobby wore a pair of his father's khaki trousers. His father is slim and the pants weren't large enough around for Bobby when he had a pillow stuffed in for padding, so they had to be spliced with string. The other children were dressed in the same sort of costumes. Little Ruth Allen, a pretty blond girl, was Snow White.

"She would look just like the Snow White in the movies if her hair was black," the children said.

Then the small company of children went marching up and down the road, visiting every house in Simpsonville. People were expecting them and had refreshments of apples or candy ready. The children sang songs and performed stunts at every place.

When they got back to Mother's, she had hot cocoa, crackers and cake ready for them, and Rob and I had our share.

NOVEMBER

TUESDAY, *November 1. Clear and cold. Heavy frost last night.* We were terribly busy all day. The dental clinic is being held tomorrow and part of next week. I went down at noon; other members of the Health Council looked after things in the morning.

The dentist works in the library, which is a room in the elementary school building. He brings a chair, an electric drill and his other tools; our county hygienist, Miss Davis, assists him. This is the fourth year he has been here and he always does very satisfactory work. He told us today that the children's teeth show decided improvement over the first years. Many of the children had never been to the dentist before then. Now it is mostly routine work with only a few cavities in the children's mouths, except for a few new children who come in each year.

Mr. Richards Bradley of Brattleboro called in the afternoon to see how we were getting along. He looks very much like a benevolent George Bernard Shaw, and has a splendid vision of what the "millennium" may become when every person working to improve health standards — from doctors to hospitals to laymen — will cooperate to form an efficient and workable system. It was largely through him, as executor of the Thompson fund, that the country's pioneer public health unit was in Windham County. He said he would never live to see it, but he hoped we younger people would work to carry out his ideas.

Thursday, November 3. Clear and chilly. The house really felt cold today and I hated to move far away from the kitchen stove, which was the only heat I had until noon, when Bob and Mr. Yates moved the chunk stove in from its summer storage quarters and set it up in the living room. I could have used the fireplace, but it takes too much time stoking it for this kind of weather. The chunk stove may not be so good as a central heating plant, but a roaring wood fire is a mighty comfortable thing on a sub-zero evening, and it is the best way I know to warm cold feet cozily.

Caroline and Royal came over this evening. The men went coon hunting. It was such a beautiful moonlight night that I wouldn't have minded going along, too, just for the sport. Instead, Caroline and I sat near the fire and sewed. I mended stockings, a job I particularly detest and cannot stand doing unless I have a special antidote in the shape of interesting conversation, so that I will hardly be conscious of what I am doing. They were all finished before the men came back, except for one pair of Bobby's golf hose which are too small for him and too large for Jean. I left those for seed, as it were.

The men saw no game and came home empty-handed.

Sunday, November 6. Very warm and sunny. We are having unusually warm, beautiful weather for November. I wouldn't object if it continued indefinitely.

After dinner we went to East Jamaica to see Francis and Gladys Colburn. They are staying at a little old farmhouse which dates back to Revolutionary times. The road to the house is narrow, built between high ledges much of the way. It is barely wide enough for one car to pass through and can be built no wider. But they had no cars in the days following the Revolution; an ox-team could get over the road comfortably.

My own great-great-great-grandparents built that house and cleared the land soon after the Revolutionary War. They came too late that first year to plant crops, but the land had to be cleared first anyway. Grandfather worked hard with his oxen, cutting down trees and burning stumps and getting the land ready to plant the following year. They had to build a tiny log cabin to live in until they could build a real house, and they had to build a barn for the stock.

But they had no money and they needed grain for their cattle and for themselves, and they needed seed to plant the following year. They wondered what to do. Grandmother was equal to that problem.

In Townshend, ten miles away, there was a grist mill. In the fall of the year the miller had more work than he could do alone, with all the farmers for miles around bringing in their grain to be ground. Grandmother got a job helping him. The miller was paid in grain and that is the way he paid Grandmother — a hundred pounds of grain a day. Sturdy Grandmother carried the grain home in a sack on her back. Ten hard miles, walking slightly bent over so the grain wouldn't slide off, added to the ten miles she traveled each day to work. And in between, long hours of lifting heavy sacks of grain, stooping and bending and lifting, with only a bright dream to sustain her.

Grandmother helped build the new house, too. It still stands there today, in the same spot, with the windows facing the long view of the West River fifty feet below the high embankment on which the house stands. The farm is in a lush, narrow valley which twists and turns with the river, but the house is built on ground high enough to be safe from floods and storms and near enough to the hills to be sheltered from the force of the winds. It must have been very grand for those days and is still comfortable and well-planned, with plenty of room for a growing family.

The barn is falling down from lack of care, but the house is now owned by a summer neighbor who has restored the interior with loving care, leaving it with all its old charm and grace. The unpainted clapboards on the outside are warped and twisted and curled by the summer sun and the winter snows. They are colored a deep mellow brown with a patina gained only by age-long struggle against the elements.

While I looked at the house and thought of the people who built it under conditions which we today would consider impossible, I wondered if we have lost something priceless which our pioneer ancestors possessed — the desire to struggle painfully toward accomplishment, the ability to overcome hardships, the will to carve out our destinies by our own efforts, unaided by bureaucrats and governments. The eight-hour working day was unheard of and would have been scoffed at as a plan fit only for soft men. And there was no place for soft men in the civilization of their day.

But to get back to the Colburns: Francis has been busy painting pictures in oil of scenes about the county. I admire his work. It is quite modern but of the type people can understand. His pictures have a ruggedness and virility which is pleasing.

I have often wondered why this age is producing painters whose main objective apparently is to portray figures with as much ruggedness and vigor and brawn as can be got into a picture. While during pioneer days when, goodness knows, many men had more of all three virtues than they have today, the paintings were fragile and light in composition.

As we drove away in the dusk, the picture which stayed in my mind was of those two people standing together outside the door of that old, old house — a delicious blending of the old and the new, with a backdrop of ageless mountains behind them.

Wednesday, November 9. Cold and cloudy, clearing in the afternoon.
This was the night of the coon supper at Caroline's and Royal's.
Caroline told us she hoped we wouldn't be too disappointed
but that, somehow, her refrigerator stopped working during
the crucial period when the raccoon was stored in it and the
meat had spoiled. In its place she had a delicious venison pie
made from meat she had canned during the summer when
Royal shot a deer in his crops. We had a splendid supper
topped off with pumpkin and apple pies. All of us ate nearly to
the bursting point, everything tasted so good.

Friday, November 11. Clear and unseasonably warm. A beautiful day.
This is Armistice Day. The twentieth anniversary of the signing
of the Armistice which was to bring peace to the world for all
time; the "war to end wars." And now there are more wars and
rumors of wars all over the face of the earth.

Mr. Yates said he remembers the first Armistice Day twenty
years ago. He said it was a dark, dismal day and the air was cold
and raw. People hardly dared to believe the wonderful news
that peace was declared.

*Saturday, November 12. Fair and warm, but very foggy in early
morning, clearing away toward noon.* The high school play, Ibsen's
"A Doll's House," was very well presented last night. In fact, it
was excellent for high school students. The part of Torvald
Helmer was especially good, done by Arseny Karpovich who
played with great feeling the difficult part of the businessman
who liked to think of his wife as a little lark flitting about with
not a care in her pretty head. Erma Eddy was Nora Helmer, his
wife. The Headmaster's two youngest children Annabelle and
Charles Pinkham were adorable as Emmy and Bob, Helmer's
children.

The County Agent had planned an interesting and varied
program for the boys and girls today. After they had their
tables set and decorated for dinner, they all went down to the
new Latchis Theater, where they were invited to explore the

place. There they saw a short movie free of charge. After that we went to the Centre Church and heard a half-hour concert on the pipe organ. The children all loved it and understood much of what it was all about. I believe they gave the classical music more attention and interest than they would have given jazz. After all, we are much more accustomed to hearing pleasant sounds and seeing beautiful scenes in nature than as if we lived in a large city.

While I was dreaming along with the music, I found myself gazing at one of the stained glass windows. A memorial window inscribed:

"In loving memory of William, Mary and Julia by their parents William P. and Mary Ann Clune."

I wondered about the story behind that: "In loving memory of William, Mary and Julia." Were they young when they died? Did they all die at once? In an epidemic? Were they the only children of William and Mary Ann? Some time soon I intend to find out.

Monday, November 14. Snow flurries in morning. Sunny in afternoon. The longest Indian Summer on record is over for this year, I imagine. The children were transported with joy this morning when they saw the snow falling and hoped it would pile up enough for sliding and skiing, but it soon stopped.

When Bobby and Jean came home tonight they had a lot to tell me about a ventriloquist who came to their school this morning. He goes around to different schools (in this county, anyway) and gives talks on health; the proper foods to make strong bodies and the way to grow strong teeth. But it was so cleverly and interestingly done that the children all gulped that part down unknowingly while they were having fun.

The ventriloquist had a big Noah and his ark, and he made the animals out of clay while the children watched. The animals talked in their own proper style (the youngsters thought) and all of them were on hand. The giraffe had such a long neck he wouldn't go through the front door so he had to go around the ark and get in the back way. Naturally, all the animals ate the best of vegetables and drank lots of milk to make them strong for the journey in the ark.

Tuesday, November 15. Snow flurries in morning, clearing during middle of day. Snow at night. The 4-H Achievement program was held tonight in the vestry of the Congregational Church, and all of us attended. The candle-lighting service at the end was as beautiful as always, and is one of the most impressive features of the yearly Achievement programs. The lights in the hall were turned out and an expectant hush fell on the audience. A match was struck and Bruce Buchanan lit a large candle.

He explained that "the large central candle stands for our 4-H club work; for long hours of working at home and on the farm, for healthful play, for planning and achieving. It speaks to us of other boys and girls in their club meetings, at fairs and picnics and camps; of State Week, Camp Waubanong and all the other events of the 4-H year. It tells us of friendships made and ambitions stirred, but most of all it calls before us pictures of our four H's." And then he asked four leaders of clubs to take the part of the H's and pass on this 4-H spirit to others.

The leaders lit smaller candles from the central candle and stood on either side of the larger flame. For a breathless moment the tiny candles flickered hesitatingly and then burned steadily, while the leaders told of the meaning of the four H's.

"Head: I pledge my head to think, to plan and to reason.

"Heart: I pledge my heart to be kind, sympathetic and true.

"Hands: I pledge my hands to be helpful, useful and skillful.

"Health: I pledge my health to enjoy life, resist disease and be efficient."

While the row of small, pointed flames burned steadily, except for a flicker now and then when someone's breath sent them wavering for a moment, the voice of Mr. Buchanan went on, telling of the meaning, the work, the need for each separate

link in the chain of light. Then the club members were invited to come forward and receive their candles. They were lighted from their leaders' flames and then the members took their places around the outside of the room in a single row, until a giant circle was formed of living flame. The room was quite bright now, lit from dozens of tiny glowing candles.

"So the light grows," the leader said, "until its beams are felt by an entire community."

Wednesday, November 16. Cloudy in early morning, clearing before noon. The men are busy getting all the odd jobs around the place done before deer hunting starts on November twenty-first. During the hunting season they never have time to do more than the daily chores, and I often carry the milk to the main road, so they can start hunting at daybreak. It's an exciting time, and hard, but they love every minute of it. For some farmers, it's the only vacation.

Rob started to put on the storm windows yesterday without washing them. He got one all fastened onto the window frame before I noticed what he was doing. I told him that I didn't want to look through a film of dust all winter whenever I looked out the windows, so reluctantly he brought them into the house and helped me wash them before putting them on.

Before the dinner dishes were done, Mother and Aunt Abbie arrived for the afternoon and evening. When the children came home from school they begged Aunt Abbie to tell some of her stories about the days of long ago, when her grandmother — the children's great-great grandmother — was alive. We all enjoy hearing her tell them, especially the one about a circuit rider, a Methodist minister, who traveled about from new settlement to new settlement on horseback, when the roads were hardly more than trails through the dense forests. The circuit riders were always Methodist ministers, she told us, who looked after the spiritual welfare of many struggling communities.

On one of his trips to Townshend this rider stopped at the same house where he always put up, dismounted from his horse and stuck his willow switch into the ground beside the hitching post. In the morning, he saddled his horse and drove away, forgetting the willow switch. Because the minister left it there, the switch was allowed to stay in the ground, where it sprouted, took root and grew. Today, it is an enormous, branching tree, one of the first trees around here to put forth new green leaves each spring.

Legend has it that the branches from the tree were cut off time after time and the wood used to make artificial limbs, and each time they were cut, the branches grew and spread more widely than ever before.

Friday, November 18. Foggy and damp. A light drizzly rain fell most of the day. Warmer and thawing. An all-day meeting of the Home Demonstration group was held at the town hall today. The meeting was scheduled to start at ten-thirty this morning but I was unable to get there before noon. Our county Home Demonstration agent met with us. She is to be married on Thanksgiving Day at the All Souls Church in Brattleboro, and she invited all of us to be at her wedding. Our group presented her with a gift of money to be used toward purchasing something she really wants and she was very much pleased. She is a tall, slender girl, three years out of college, with dark brown hair and pretty hazel eyes.

She told us about a conference in London next year of country women from all over the world. It is called The Conference of the Associated Country Women of the World. Each state in the United States hopes to send several delegates. It would be a wonderful experience, meeting women from every country in the world, all of whom have similar interests, and all of them trying to work out problems together. A wider acquaintance with farm women of our times should help to secure more effective cooperation, and show a way to improve home conditions throughout the world. The last such conference was held at Cornell University in Ithaca, New York, two years ago.

Our leader went on to say that Windham County hoped to send a delegate and that the Advisory Committee of the Farm Bureau had already discussed possible candidates and that they would like to see one of our group in Townshend go as delegate; in short, one Muriel Follett. Of course, all the Home Demonstration groups in the county would have to vote for the delegate they wanted to send, but she hoped I wouldn't mind her mentioning it for the first time in an open meeting.

Mind? I didn't know what to think. It was flabbergasting, to put it inelegantly. I hadn't thought of such a thing being possible for me. It sounded like something too good to be true. Something one dreams about for years without much expecting it to happen.

It's still a long way from being a probability. It would take four or five hundred dollars, according to the itinerary of the trip, and that is a lot of money to raise in our county for anything outside of necessities. And . . . oh, so many things might happen. But if there is a possibility of going, I'll work like everything to help it come true. Just think of it! It would be like a dream come alive!

Of course, there would be a few "incidentals" beside, like clothes and luggage and things like that, but they could be managed somehow. Anyway, I'll pray for world peace with greater zeal than ever before.

Saturday, November 19. Rain, becoming heavier and colder toward night. Jean has found a painless way to make Bobby help her with the dishes. She is an inordinate reader and reads so fast I wonder whether she can remember it all. I had a chance to find out today. She was washing dishes and telling fairy stories to Bobby while he wiped the dishes. She did a complete job of it,

191

too. Bobby listened spellbound and wiped away without a murmur.

"You know," Bobby whispered to me when Jean wasn't looking, "you know, I just love to hear Jean tell stories, but don't tell her so, will you?"

"Why not? If someone thought you were doing something well, wouldn't you like to be told about it?"

"Ye-es," hesitantly, "but I'd hate to make Jean stuck up."

"You don't need to worry," I assured Bobby. "Why don't you tell her you like to hear her tell stories. She would appreciate it."

"We-ell, maybe. Gee, she *does* tell swell stories."

Later, I overheard Bobby say, "Tell another story, will you Jean? That last one you told was interesting."

The annual meeting of the Co-operative Milk Plant was held today in Brattleboro. Rob and I went down. Some fine reports were given. It was reported that our plant pays more for milk at the present time than any other co-op in the state.

The dinner served was especially good and the farmers stowed away a surprising amount. There were big bowls of oyster stew followed by baked beans, sour-milk biscuits and cheese. Then thick slabs of delicious ice cream with small cookies, and coffee. The helpings were generous and seconds of everything were served to all who wanted more. All of us were slightly overstuffed when we left the tables. Because of that, the afternoon program droned along slowly with many heads nodding. It must have been a trying audience for the speaker.

Tuesday, November 22. Warm and sunny. Rob persuaded me that today would be a good day to spend deer hunting with him and the rest of the gang. Although I arose soon after five I was unable to get around at daybreak as they did. Anyway, I don't like to leave before the children go to school. Maybe I am old-fashioned and all that, but I remember how I liked to have my mother around when I left for school. It gave me a feeling of permanence, of rightness in my world. My children feel the same way. They always call to me when they come home and they hunt the house over for me, calling as they go, if they don't find me at once. If I can give them that feeling of stability by just being around when they need me, it will be something gained in this chaotic world which they must enter in a few more years. Every person needs a haven, a place where he is needed and made to feel important, and why should parents hesitate to give a few hours, out of a lifetime of hours, to the important building of happiness? At least, that is the way I feel about it.

But to return to the hunt, I was all ready to go when the school bus arrived for the children. A few minutes later, my brothers stopped for me on their way from the west woods to the big woods southeast of the house.

The day was unusually warm for the last of November and a heavy sweater over two light ones was enough, so I left my heavy jacket at home. I wore leather snow boots over ski pants, but I wished afterward that I had put on rubbers, for while there was little snow and water near the house, the hills and valleys in the woods simply oozed moisture. No one should mistake me for a deer, with a bright blue sweater above navy pants, a red cap and red wool socks. My lunch was slung in a pouch fastened to my belt, a hunting knife hung over my right hip. My gun was a pleasing weight in the crook of my arm.

I sincerely hoped that there would be no reason for using that knife. If I shot a deer, I hoped someone else would be there to stick it and dress it off, but in a tight pinch the knife might come in handy. I've watched the process many times and know how it is done, but it's not an appealing operation, and I am willing to have someone else do it.

The best part of a day in the woods is not, however, the thought of the kill. It is the tangy air, the heady, warming sunshine, the steady thump of a good heart as it quickens its beat to accommodate a climber. It is all these things and many more. Intangible things like the thrill of seeing a partridge rise under your feet with a loud thrumming of its wings, the beauty of watching lazy clouds drift across a rich blue sky. It is an awakening of all your senses into a coordinating whole. You breathe more deeply, hear more clearly, and try to analyze each separate sound.

Is that noise in the underbrush to your left a deer? No — it's only dried birch leaves rustling in a vagrant breeze. But you see a motion in the woods in front of you . . . Looking closely, you see a small red squirrel scurrying about in the dead leaves.

And so it goes. Always something that might prove exciting; always the suspense, the waiting, attuning mind and body to something only half understood.

Then, finally, after long waiting — you hear a sound advancing toward you. Is it a deer or one of your gang, driving through the woods? Wait . . . it sounds like . . . no (settling back faintly disappointed), it wears a red coat and walks on two legs. The drive is over. Well, maybe next time, on the next drive. . . .

In the meantime, I like the thought of not being alone, knowing there are other hunters within reach of my voice. I am not a timid sort of person and I can use my gun handily, but along with the peaceful animals like squirrels and rabbits and deer, I know there are bobcats and occasionally bears. If one of these should just happen to sneak up behind me and jump on my neck, I'd like to be able to yell, "Help!" — and get it.

On the second drive, I stood on top of a hill on a long moss-grown ledge. A small spruce tree only a few feet higher than my head was acting as a shield from curious woods' eyes. All around were numerous giant Christmas trees, many forty-five or fifty feet high, kept in constant motion by a brisk wind. I thought how beautiful they would look when decked out with silver snow or long icicles on each one of their branches. The sun was warm and I took off my gloves, unwrapped a sandwich and started to eat it.

There was a sound in the shallow gully at my right but I

couldn't see. . . . The sandwich dropped, forgotten, beside my gloves. I sneaked softly over the mossy ledge and peered down into the gully. The sun shone into my eyes and partly blinded me. I crept along the ledge until I stood in the shadow of a tall spruce, cocking my gun silently as I went. Down in a ravine was a deer, hugging close to the hillside and working back away from the lower hunter he had seen or smelled. The wind was against my face so he couldn't get my scent and he didn't see me. It *looked* like a buck. I was sure of it, but in the underbrush I could see no horns. How was I sure? A buck is shaped different- ly from a doe; he walks differently, as a stallion has a different swing to his body than a mare.

All the time, he was working his way leisurely back over the brow of the hill, keeping in the thick underbrush. When he got beyond me and out of sight I decided to try to head him off. He might come out in the open if I waited, but then again he might not.

I stepped around the spreading branches of the spruce tree and saw him coming a second later than he saw me. With a shake of his hooves and a flash of his flag he disappeared into the woods, toward where Jim was standing.

"Look out," I yelled, and waited.

Then there was a shot. Another. "Jim got him," I thought. And he had.

I went back to my sandwiches and gloves. Somewhat later, I heard a movement in the same ravine but I sat quietly in front of the little spruce tree, waiting, with my hands gripping the gun.

Slowly, oh so slowly and cautiously, the rustling sound contin- ued. I saw something move low down over the edge of the long ledge. I hardly breathed. Then a deer stepped out into the open space below me. I knew in a minute that it was an old doe bigger than many bucks but I still sat motionless, curious to know what she would do. She didn't see me and she kept coming. Finally, she worked her way around a big bull spruce tree hardly more than twenty yards away. Then she saw me. Her head came up, her whole body stiffened to attention and her ears bent forward. She stood there staring at me while I stared back. For several minutes we watched each other while she made up her mind about me. Then she whirled like a flash and was gone. I knew by the careful way she had come that she was an advance guard for something. It might have been her mate. But Rob said, later, that he had seen her before and she had two half-grown fawns with her.

It was a thrilling experience and I wouldn't have missed it — the doe's incredible grace and wariness, her curiosity and speed, in the bright sun on the hilltop, with a background of deep green trees.

Wednesday, November 23. Cloudy in morning. Snow and sleet in afternoon and evening. Colder. The pleasure of this business of early rising in the cold, small hours before dawn does *not* grow on one. I am already fed up with it. I could have done with more sleep this morning, and I stretched and yawned vigorously for some time before I could persuade my tired muscles to obey the dictates of my mind.

There is always that mad rush of scrambling into clothes, rushing out to the kitchen to stoke a lagging wood fire and hurrying to start breakfast for the hungry multitude. Muffins have to be made, a large double boiler full of hot cereal prepared, coffee made, tomato juice poured, the table set and so forth, on and on. In the lull that follows the family's rush to the dining room table I must get out the material for sandwiches and start getting lunches ready to be taken to the woods.

Making sandwiches is easier this year than last because of the smaller volume necessary. Last year, I had forty or fifty sandwiches to prepare before the first break of dawn. This year, there are not quite so many hunters to feed. Nevertheless, I have to hurry to get the lunches put up in the proper shapes and sizes and wrapped carefully to fit each hunter's individual pockets.

The children are usually getting up by this time and are trying to find a warm, sheltered corner in which to dress, and the hunters are trying to locate and sort out a hundred-and-one articles of wearing apparel; coats, hats, mittens, sweaters and ear muffs from around the kitchen stove, where they were left to dry the night before. If I try to wade through this welter of humanity and wraps I become lost in the shuffle. I usually subside against one of the seven doors in the kitchen and wait until the guns are loaded, with their muzzles pressed against the kitchen floor, and boxes of cartridges are put back on any convenient resting place (except the stove). Then, the sky having lightened, the hunters trail out through open doors carrying their guns under their arms. Usually several of them trickle back to pick up forgotten mittens or lunches.

With the kitchen cleared (comparatively speaking), I realize that the fire is nearly out, that there are a lot of dirty dishes to be washed and — that I am hungry. Not only hungry but tired, and the day's work not yet begun.

Rob got a deer today. A large spike horn, weighing 113 pounds, dressed.

Thursday, November 24. Much colder. 16 degrees above zero at dawn. Thanksgiving Day. The men wanted to spend the day in the woods as usual so we had Thanksgiving dinner at night. It has been our custom during the past few years to have Thanksgiving at my home and Christmas at Mother's or at my brother Donald's in Athens. We are such a large family that all of us cannot get together at once so we divide up the two holidays. I had eleven for dinner tonight. Sometimes there are fifteen or sixteen.

Mother and my sister-in-law, Velma, came early in the afternoon and helped with the preparation of the dinner. I had made four pumpkin pies in the morning and Mother brought two mince pies and some cranberry sauce.

A hunter came to the door this afternoon trying to find his

direction. He didn't know whether he had left his car in Brookline, Newfane or Townshend. He had wandered over several back roads before he came to our house and he wanted to know how to get back to his car.

"I followed my friend's automobile this morning," he said, "and I didn't notice landmarks much. I just followed him."

For nearly half an hour I tried to help him discover where he left his automobile but it was no use. He kept repeating, "I am all turned around." Finally I showed him the way back to Brookline, which seemed the most probable place for his car to be. I wonder if he managed to get home safely.

When the day began to darken into evening, the men returned from the woods. By that time snow had begun to fall and the wind was blowing a gale. The temperature was dropping rapidly. Snow swirled and eddied about the house. But Father had a deer. I am glad it was he who got it.

Rob and his brothers, Jim and John, took the deer down to the town clerk's office to report it and stopped on the way back to do Father's chores. Father stayed here.

Dinner was nearly ready, and Mother was fixing the squash when Father came into the kitchen to watch us.

"How much sweetening do you put in the squash?" Mother asked me.

"Probably about two gul-lups," Father answered for me. "You've heard that story, haven't you?" We hadn't.

"It seems," Father began, his deep-set gray eyes twinkling quietly, "it seems that years ago Martha Brigham was telling a friend of hers the recipe for a dish of something she had just made. She said she added two gul-lups of molasses.

"How much is a gul-lup?" her friend wanted to know.

"Well, you know when you tip a jug of molasses up to let it run out it goes, 'gul-lup' with a hiccoughing noise. My recipe calls for two gul-lups."

It was a nice Thanksgiving. We finished our coffee in the living room because the Amos 'n' Andy program came on and all of us wanted to know whether Andy managed to wrangle a Thanksgiving dinner out of his friends without having to cut in. It was a satisfying conclusion when Andy had not one, but three Thanksgiving dinners, and thought he ought to change his vest between places so he wouldn't carry gravy from one house to another.

Late in the evening after the others had gone and the children were in bed, Uncle Rob and Rob sat before the fire talking of hunting and fishing and land and timber while I watched and listened.

DECEMBER

*S*UNDAY, *December 4. Sunny and warm like spring weather.* The day couldn't have been more pleasant — unless one wanted to get somewhere. Overhead, the bright sun shone warm in a deep blue sky. Underfoot, the roads were awful, better fitted for huge skating rinks than to drive upon. The rain of yesterday which froze as it fell, left fields and highways a glittering mass of glare ice. Unfortunately, they were too tip-tilted to skate upon in the usual manner, with skates, but only a cool-headed, experienced driver could keep from sliding into ditches or over banks with an automobile.

Rob and his father were away all day with the truck, collecting livestock. The children and I were planning to go to church with Mother in her car but Rob telephoned from a neighbor's house, after they had gone about a mile over the slippery roads, to say that they weren't safe for travel and that discouraged us. It was just as well, I suppose, because several cars got stuck on the turn at the foot of Popl' Tree Hill and had to have help getting out.

Rob bought a dozen head of purebred, registered Holstein cattle today in the northern part of the state. At least there will be a dozen, we expect, when the last cows freshen and their offspring arrive. There are seven milking cows and a young bull, beside the calves. He brought home two of them in the truck. They are beautiful animals, and we hope they will swell the milk check which we are getting from our Guernseys until we will be able to see it. Golden Guernsey milk is tops so far as I am concerned, but quantity counts more than a high butterfat test at our cooperative milk plant. All of us are excited over the new cows. Rob plans to milk them three times daily at eight hour intervals.

Milk producers who milk three times a day instead of twice claim that they get a third more milk from their cows. (The extra work involved ought to bring *some* results.) Rob thinks that the hours most convenient for him to milk will be at midnight, 8:00 A.M. and 4:00 P.M. But how convenient is *that!*

Monday, December 5. Rainy and slippery. The view from the dining room windows was exquisite, early this morning. Every branch and twig and fir tree was ribbed with crystal frost. They looked like huge confections and were almost unbelievably beautiful. Fog was thick in the valleys but the day had a pearly luster, seen only in winter, and we thought the fog would clear as soon as the sun came out.

Other people thought so, too. John Follett and a gang of men arrived early, planning to put a new roof on the barn today. There were about ten men and they expected to finish it today. By the time they arrived here, a misty rain had started to fall, which froze onto the roof and ladders and working equipment. It would have been dangerous to attempt the job, so they left until the next fair day, when the weather is not too cold and the barn roof is not covered with snow. The barn ought to have been roofed earlier in the fall, but we were hindered by this and that.

Father shipped his calves today from a train siding twenty-five miles distant. He didn't dare to drive the truck, so Rob drove for him again today. They had two loads to take. I can remember when Father used to collect calves from all the towns within a radius of fifteen or twenty miles, on a Saturday, with horses and a long sled. (Automobiles couldn't travel over the winter hill roads then.) Then on the next Monday, he would carry all the calves on a sled to the station, twenty-five miles from home. That was a long jaunt for horses, and often Father didn't get home until nearly midnight. It is better now, even with slippery roads.

Tuesday, December 6. Cloudy in morning. Rain fell heavily all night and continued most of the morning. The brooks were high, and we could hear the rushing roar of our usually timid little brook at the foot of the hill when we were in the house with all the doors and windows closed.

Rob knew how much I wanted to attend the Book Fair at Brattleboro this afternoon and evening so he never even suggested that we ought to stay home. Rain was falling at noon when we started, and it continued to fall until we were nearly in Brattleboro. Mother was planning to go with us but the rain discouraged her.

"I don't know whether we will be able to get home," Rob said. "If the rain continues, the roads will be flooded."

He was right, for the low river banks through Townshend and Newfane were already full and beginning to overflow onto the surrounding meadows, and the water from the little streams in the hills would continue to swell the river for some time after the rain had ceased. We decided to take a chance on things being all right, anyway.

I love fairs and especially book fairs. In fact, I like to talk to people and watch them so much that it is difficult to concentrate on the books. Really to enjoy books, one needs plenty of solitude and time, to read little snatches here and there in each, to study the names of the authors and their individual styles. Yes, books are fascinating — but so are people — and one expects the books will be available after the people have gone. It is rather confusing but altogether delightful.

The speakers of the afternoon had such varied interests and aims that one was able to get a well rounded and comprehensive idea of what books mean, not only to the author and casual reader, but to the publishers, the bookmakers, the booksellers and to the scholars who pass on their learning to students in classrooms.

At the close of the afternoon I wanted to stay on through the evening program. But Rob had to get back home, and without him, I didn't know how I would get there. It was then that I learned all over again the value of good friends. Mrs. Buchanan said warmly,

"Of course you must stay down this evening. Come out to our house with us and stay to supper, and I have a couch in my living room that is just begging for company for the night. Spend the night with us and you can go home on the bus in the morning."

Now Mrs. Buchanan has boarders and her family is about fifteen strong without extras. That is about enough for an ordinary person, but her heart is as warm and big as the noonday sun.

The evening program rounded out the entire book fair in a most satisfying manner and then the last speaker, David Morton, a poet — tall, scholarly, yet physically stalwart — recited from his own poems, a moving picture of the gifts of beauty which each New England season brings; "spring, tentative and slow, full-blown summer, the golden season that follows, and the naked grandeurs and stark austerities of winter." The poetry was full of poignant meaning to those of us conscious of seasonal changes and David Morton's voice was smooth and fine, flowing along in the apparently effortless symmetry that poetry needs.

The Dauchys were down from Townshend for the evening session, so I rode home with them as far as the village. They said they would telephone Rob to come after me, but he was asleep and didn't hear the telephone. I didn't mind. In fact, the night had cleared and was just right for walking. The air was crisp and clean-washed.

The moon, almost full, reflected on the snow, made glittering jewels of the hills and valleys. "She walks in beauty," I quoted to myself and then, irrelevantly, "I wish I had on my walking shoes instead of dress shoes."

Nevertheless, the three and a half miles seemed short and I felt only happily tired and relaxed as I reached home. Rob was surprised when I got into bed beside him. He asked me where I came from.

"From Heaven," I answered sleepily.

Wednesday, December 7. Fair in morning, cloudy in afternoon. The men came to roof the barn this morning. They ought to finish it tomorrow. There is a lot of surface to cover. The barn is 120 feet by 40 feet and has a hip roof.

Mother was going to Brattleboro to do some Christmas shopping this morning and she asked me to go with her. I didn't have time to do any shopping yesterday, so I was glad to go. We will have to go down again later to finish up and we plan to go when the children will be out of school and able to come with us.

They are busy practicing for Christmas services at school and at the church. Bobby is to sing a solo and Jean sings with the group. They are supposed to represent child angels and the girls need white dresses and the boys white shirts and trousers. All the boys' white trousers were too short for their fast-growing bodies, so they will wear white robes to cover their dark clothes. Jean had no white dress either so I will have to make her one.

Friday, December 9. Showers all day. Warm. The snow is almost gone, and the roads are as muddy and slippery as they are in the spring.

The Home Demonstration group met today with Eloise Carleton and Mrs. Brown. They live in the same house, one in the upstairs apartment and one downstairs. The whole house was opened up, the covered-dish dinner was served upstairs and the meetings were held downstairs. It was a nice arrangement and made enough room for the good-sized crowd.

We were all supposed to wear old-fashioned clothes and there were clothes from all periods during the last hundred years. Many were beautiful and all were interesting. We told the history of each costume as far as we knew it. I wore a long tan linen duster and a little pancake hat, much the same style as those of today, made of pleated brown velvet and decorated with an ecru lace rosette.

The group has already raised some money which is to be used for the delegate's trip to the Country Women's Conference in London, next June, and we are anxious to raise more. As time goes on it looks more probable that I might be able to go. I ought to *know* for sure pretty soon since there are many things to be done before that time.

Saturday, December 10. More rain. Rob began last night to milk the cows three times a day. He went to bed early and arose at eleven-thirty to do his midnight milking. One of the new heifers had a heifer calf at that time, so Rob took quite some time looking after her. She was very thirsty and Rob had to heat two pans full of hot water for her, and then give her some hot bran mash. She promises to be a fine cow and one has to use care with high-producing animals, even above that usually given.

The little new calf belongs to Jean. It is still with its mother in a pen, but Jean loves to look in through the boards of the pen and pet the calf when it comes near enough. She is making big plans for its future.

During his spare time at the barn Bobby "gentles" the cattle. He has the new ones trained so they stretch out their heads for him to scratch, as he goes past. The little Holstein bull will do more for Bobby than anyone else in the barn, although Bobby is trained never to take chances with bulls because they cannot be trusted.

We have been making Christmas presents today. The children made toy owls for their cousins, Louise and Betty Jane, and have made up Christmas cards for their friends. Jean even made up her own poems to print on the cards.

Monday, December 12. I woke up at three this morning with the feeling that something was not just as it should be.

"Rob," I said, "did you get up for the midnight milking?"

He was wide awake in an instant. "Lord, no. What time is it?"

"Three o'clock."

"Do you suppose that damned alarm didn't go off?"

He reached over to the alarm clock, which sat on a chair far enough from the bed so he had to uncover his arms and shoulders to get it. He turned the stem that winds the alarm.

"Run down," he muttered. "Didn't you hear it go off, either?"

"Not a sound."

"Lord, I wouldn't have had that happen for a good deal. Those cows should have been milked three hours ago. Well, the only thing to do is to milk them now." Soon, I heard him rattling the fires and putting in more wood. And then the clank of milk pails and the closing of the kitchen door as he left for the barn.

I snuggled into the blankets until I thought the fires would be going well and then got up. It was an unearthly hour, but I was wide awake. It was a nice quiet time to write before the children stirred and I had to stop to get breakfast.

Rob left at seven to get the last two cows. He was gone until

three this afternoon. The roads were bad and the dirt roads were muddy. He almost got stuck several times.

I spent all the morning after the children left and the work was done making Jean's white dress. It takes more time to make than some dresses because it is shirred and ruffled.

History was made in Lima, Peru, today, according to news dispatches. Secretary Hull's speech this morning was credited with setting the keynote of the conference, where twenty-one republics in the Americas have decided to show a united front to the rest of the world and hold fast to peace and Democracy.

I hope this confab will mean something more than idle, meaningless chatter. It remains to be proved whether the Americas can keep their word better than the majority of European countries today. It is a magnificent gesture, and we all hope it does some good.

People in general don't want war today. What mother of sons has ever wanted war? And what has it ever accomplished?

The women of the world are waking up to their own individual responsibilities and place in the world's scheme of things. Next spring, at the Conference of Associated Country Women of the World in London, they plan to attempt to cement firm friendships with women of many countries. One such conference wouldn't bring about all the things people desire, but several, over a period of years, might do much good. Anyway, what have men been able to accomplish? It is time women took a hand in things.

It would be a thrilling thing to be a small part in such a world conference, to meet and learn to understand the women and their problems, their hopes and goals. To see their countries and be able to compare them at first hand, with ours.

My county, Windham County, in Vermont, still plans to send a delegate to that conference and I may be that delegate. It would be a tremendous responsibility both during the conference and after, when I tried to bring back to the people at home what I had learned, but I am thrilled at the possibility of going. I won't know for sure whether I can go for a month or two yet.

Wednesday, December 14. Mostly cloudy. Snow flurries at night. Bobby's Sunday School Class had a "working party" this evening at the home of Betty Morse, one of the members. Ruby Capen is their teacher and she had them make costumes for Christmas. The members of the class are going to hand out the presents at the Community Christmas Tree next week Thursday after Santa Claus reads off the names.

Every child in town, from infants through the eight grades in school, receives some gift. All of them get an orange and each child up to four years of age has a present; the older ones have boxes of candy. The shut-ins are remembered, too, with baskets of fruit.

Thursday, December 15. Fair. Much colder. Rob finally woke up last night for the midnight milking, but it took the combined efforts of the alarm clock and me to rouse him — and how I hated to do it! I heard the alarm whirr and sputter and finally choke to a stop as it ran down. Rob stirred and then settled back to sleep until I shook him and called his name. The night was cold and I shivered until he came back to bed again.

Another calf was born yesterday. The baby weighed a hundred pounds or more. A sizable baby for any animal and the poor cow was as relieved as any human mother when it was over.

Saturday, December 17. Cloudy in early morning, snow flurries and rain in late morning and afternoon. We had promised Bobby and Jean a trip to Brattleboro before Christmas and today seemed the best time to go, since school keeps until the day before Christmas. We decided to start early to avoid the worst of the Saturday's rush and we were ready by eight-thirty. We went with Mother in her car.

The children had their own money and weeks ago had made

out careful lists of the people for whom they wanted to buy presents. They had to plan carefully to make their money stretch over gifts for all our many relatives. They had already made several gifts at home and plan to make some more before Christmas.

I wonder if the salesgirls in the store where we did most of our shopping, were aware of the secret excitement going on all around them. One or two of them seemed to catch some of it and looked thrilled and interested. To the others, the work was merely a hard routine.

Bobby and Jean wanted help selecting some of their gifts. First Jean would whisper, "Please come with me a minute and don't let Bobby tag along." Then Bobby would motion to me to leave Jean behind while I offered him advice on his present to Jean. Mother helped the children select my gift (that leaked out in spite of all their secrecy), and I helped them select her gift. It was grand fun even though it did mean lots of traveling back and forth and hurried purchases of my own. I wish we could give much more, but we might not have more real enjoyment and pleasure in Christmas than we do now, when we have to plan so carefully and put more of ourselves into our gifts.

Big, white Christmasy-looking flakes of snow began to fall toward noon and all the people looked so nice and dressed-up with the snow clinging to their hats and coats and making wet splotches on their faces. It was the clinging-est sort of snow and it sort of caressed one when it landed. It fell only long enough to cover the streets and trees with a thin layer of white and then stopped for a while.

We got home shortly after noon and after we had eaten our lunch and the children had changed into play clothes, Bobby persuaded Jean to go with him after our Christmas tree and another one for Mother. (The persuasion was accomplished by Bobby's helping Jean wash the dishes.) Bobby had found our tree months before and had marked it for now. Spruce trees which grow in open land usually have thicker branches and are better rounded, and this one is a beauty. Mother wanted a smaller one for her smaller room and they found one they thought would satisfy her, too.

Bobby had never made a standard for the Christmas tree before but he went at it like an old hand. The tree was too tall for our living room so he measured the height of the room and cut what he thought was enough off the base of the tree. He forgot to allow for the height of the standard, however, and we are wondering tonight whether to let the tall top spike of the tree bend over on the ceiling or to take off the standard again and cut more from the trunk of the tree.

Jean took the lovely, curved branches which were cut off the base of the tree and made beautiful decorations for our doors.

The tree they got for Mother looked rather scraggly beside ours, and Bobby intends to get a better one for her. Jean wanted to use this one for the birds' Christmas presents. I gave her some suet and she hung it high in the tree. But not high enough. Sammy Dog thought it was meant for him and had a small Christmas feast of his own before she caught him.

Tonight, Bobby said,

"Mother, do you suppose we will do this year what we usually do?"

"What is that?"

"Don't you know? We usually wake up about two o'clock Christmas morning and say, 'Mother, can't I get up? Can't I get up?' and we don't sleep much after that."

"I don't believe you will this year, do you? After all, you are old enough now to wait until a reasonable time before you get up to look at your stockings and presents."

"But it's such fun. I always hate to wait. Do you remember when we always left something for Santa Claus to eat on the mantel over the fireplace. Now, please tell us, wasn't it Daddy who ate the food?"

"— and do you remember," Jean chimed in, "do you remember when we set a dish of water on the hearth stone so

Santa could wash the soot from the chimney off his hands before he ate the lunch. And how black the water was in the morning? Did Daddy do that?"

"What do *you* think?" I hedged.

Sunday, December 18. Snow. Warmer. Snow fell slowly today, in great soft flakes. The trees and shrubs and stone walls look like a scene from fairyland — or Christmas time. Every branch and twig and stone is outlined "inch deep with pearl," against a base which looks black by comparison.

I wish I could paint a picture of the bare maple tree which stands at the corner of our big red barn. Its white-ribbed branches stand out like delicate tracery against the redness of the high barn. The air is still and the damp snow sticks fast to the branches and bends them down with its weight.

Although the world was cool and majestic outside, there was warmth and a quiet bustle going on inside the house, which swelled at times to a quick crescendo when the children became excited over the Christmas tree or something they were planning for Christmas.

Bobby decided that the tree must be perfect, so he took off the standard again and cut several more inches from its base. He had difficulty in getting it back together again and his Dad went out into the shed to help him. Soon, I heard loud laughter. Bobby came in and said,

"Daddy tried to show me how it should be done and then he had the same trouble I did."

But all that makes for companionship.

The tree was nice when it was set up in its corner of the living room. It fitted as if it had always belonged there. Bobby was proud of his work, as he well should be. They wanted to trim it right away, but we needed help cracking butternuts for maple butternut candy. We don't plan to do that kind of work on Sundays, but our work had rushed us until this was the only time we could work together to make the candy. And that is a job we have always done together, Rob and I. Probably we could do it alone, but when the maple sugar has been boiled to the right consistency, and cooled and stirred until the last minute possible before it hardens, then we both are rushed and busy getting the luscious mass into the rubber leaf and heart molds in time for it to harden smoothly.

Today, we wanted to add butternuts for extra goodness, and that is where the children helped.

Later, when the candy was hardened, we took it out of the molds and packed it into bright-colored glassine cups and then into boxes and covered it all with cellophane to keep it fresh and sweet.

Tonight, the children have gone to bed. But the tree is already trimmed and it holds some gifts. Jean wanted terribly to show me the present she got for me.

"It is right there on the Christmas tree any time you want to peek," she told me.

"I'll *try* to hold out until Christmas," I answered, "although I am anxious to know what you have for me."

"I hope you'll like it. Grandma thought you would."

"Oh, oh, hold on," Bobby warned her. "In just another minute you will be telling her."

"I would *like* to," wistfully. "Mother, don't you want to know . . . ?"

"Of course I do, but don't you think we'd better wait?"

"Ye-es, I suppose so," reluctantly, "but I don't see how I'm going to."

Tuesday, December 20. Colder. Partly cloudy. The children practiced their Christmas songs for me to hear, this evening, and after they had gone to bed Christmas carols came in over the radio and I turned it louder so they could hear. Those songs never grow old. I tell the children how fortunate they are to be able to sing them. In Germany, Christmas is outlawed and only Yule remains. Yule may be historic, but it is not soul-satisfying, and,

I believe, people in dictator-governed countries still need beauty — and hope and peace.

Wednesday, December 21. Partly cloudy. The children came home from the village tonight lugging a big Christmas package from their Great-Uncle John and Aunt Florence. He is one of their favorite uncles and he has a consistent way of making children happy, so Bobby and Jean wanted to open the package right away, more than anything else they could think of.

"You'd better wait until Christmas morning," I told them.

"But Mother, can't we just take off the outside wrappings and take out the presents. They are all wrapped up. I — I looked where the wrapping paper was torn." Bobby looked a little guilty, but eager.

"But what good would it do if you saw the outside of the packages. You wouldn't know what was inside."

"We could shake them a little," Jean said hopefully.

"Would that be fair?" I asked.

"No, maybe not. . . . I'll tell you what we will do. The packages would look nice on the Christmas tree and if you will let us put them on the tree we will promise not to peek inside them, won't we, Jean?"

"Yes, yes," Jean pleaded. "We will promise not to peek."

"Well," I weakened, "I don't see that it will do you much good but if you won't peek. . . ."

And so the packages were lifted from their wrapping paper and put on the tree. There was a little surreptitious shaking, but nothing rattled and they were done up beautifully and securely.

"I don't see how I can wait," Jean said, jumping up and down with excitement, "but I have to, somehow. I promised not to peek and I won't."

Everything considered, they do better than many older folks. I know because I . . . well . . . *skip* it!

The children haven't seen the other packages which have arrived. I put them away carefully where they won't find them, I hope.

214

"It is hard enough to wait," Jean said, "when we are going to school and our mind is taken up with other things, but it is going to be terrible on Saturday, when we are home all day. And we have a solid session Friday morning and we will be home all the afternoon. I don't know what we will do with ourselves."

Bobby went shopping for the rest of his Christmas gifts today, during his school recess. When the children got home from school this afternoon, he came up to me and said urgently,

"Now don't say anything, Mother, please. I've *got* to show you what I bought for you, right now."

It surprised me so I couldn't have said anything, anyway. He had a set of the cutest salt-and-pepper shakers shaped like diminutive owls.

Thursday, December 22. Fair and colder. The road men are working on the road that goes past our house. It is cold work, but I hope they can get the road in shape to plow when we have more snow that needs plowing. Now, there are only three or four inches and it is packed down hard. The hills that were slippery have been sanded.

We all went down to the Community Christmas Tree this evening. I thought the program was unusually good. It was mostly composed of Christmas songs, with a few other numbers worked in by the primary grades.

Hazel and her two children sat with Rob and me. Jeannette, who is not quite three, was looking forward to seeing Santa Claus and kept asking for him. I don't believe she had ever seen him before. Finally, as the last song was finished, Santa came up the stairs in the rear of the town hall, with sleigh bells ringing and a hearty "hello."

Unexpectedly, Jeannette covered her face with her tiny hands and began to cry with fright. And she couldn't be comforted.

Bobby and Jean put the gifts they received on our Christmas

tree. Both youngsters received Beano games. Bobby had one before, and he had decided to give this one away to someone else until he discovered the name of the giver inside the box. It was from the girl in his class whom he likes best.

"I wouldn't give it away now, for anything," he said, "and I was just planning to ask *her* if she would like a Beano game. O-oh, what if I had? Gosh!"

"She isn't my girl friend," he explained carefully, "she is merely the girl I like best in school. There's a difference."

Saturday, December 24. Cloudy. Light snow. We are sure to have a white Christmas this year in spite of predictions to the contrary.

The children found switches in their stockings this morning, one in each of the stockings which hang by the fireplace ready for Santa. But they weren't wholly unprepared. Rob brought the switches in last night after he thought the children were in bed, but Bobby was slow getting ready and he still sat in a chair in the kitchen, talking, when Rob opened the door.

Rob thought he had hidden them under his coat so Bobby wouldn't see them, as he came into the kitchen and went on into the dining room. But Bobby had noticed his dad's start of surprise when he opened the door and wanted to know all about it. He followed his father into the dining room in time to see the switches being hidden.

"Oh, ho, I'll bet you cut those to put in our stockings," said Bobby.

"Why, how you talk," said his dad. "Now, leave those arrows alone," he warned, as Bobby started to reach for them.

After he had gone to bed I heard him talking to Jean and telling her all about it. "But don't let on that you know anything about it," he cautioned.

We planned to keep busy during the day so the time would pass as quickly as possible. Bobby and Jean helped with the work, but their minds weren't on what they were doing, as the halfway results showed. They had to practice for the Caroler's program at the church tomorrow night, and I took them and June Brown down to the village this afternoon.

The Federated Church holds services half the year in the Congregational Church and the other half year, during the winter, services are held in the Baptist Church. Roy Severance, a young man who graduated from high school last June, directed the program, and he had also decorated the Baptist church very beautifully with woodsy greens and red streamers and white lilies. Erma Eddy, a senior in high school, played the organ, as she does nearly every Sunday. They were helped by another high school senior, Leota Styles.

These young people were training the younger children from six years of age to fifteen years for an evening's program of Christmas carols. They were doing a fine job of it, too, a job that would have done credit to any older group, with more experience.

At night, Jean said,

"It doesn't seem as if I ever saw a day so long as this one has been. I wonder if Christmas will ever come."

They have heard again the *Letter to Virginia* ("Yes, Virginia, there *is* a Santa Claus") which they hear nearly every Christmas, and the Bible story of the birth of the Christ Child:

"And there were in the same country shepherds abiding in the field, keeping watch over their flocks by night. And lo, the angel of the Lord came upon them, and the glory of the Lord shone round about them: and they were sore afraid. And the angel said unto them, Fear not: for behold, I bring you good tidings of great joy, which shall be to all people. For unto you is born this day in the city of David a Savior, which is Christ the Lord."

Christmas Day, December 25. Warmer. Partly cloudy. The few inches of fresh, light snow which fell yesterday covered the bare spots where the old snow had melted away and made a mantle of loveliness for Christmas Day.

When Rob got up for his twelve o'clock milking last night Bobby called,

"Daddy, is it time to get up?"

"No, it is only midnight. Go back to sleep."

Later, this morning, when both Bobby and Jean were up, looking at their stockings and the gifts on their Christmas tree, Bobby remarked,

"I wanted awfully to get up when Daddy did last night, and look at my presents, but I controlled myself."

"I think this is the happiest Christmas I ever had," Jean said excitedly as she danced about. "Then, that is what I thought last year. But last year is past now."

"I wish everybody in the whole world was as happy as I am," Bobby remarked thoughtfully.

Our friends and relatives remembered us generously. The children had a number of nice books like Felix Salten's *Perri* and James Fenimore Cooper's *The Spy;* and Rob and I were presented with subscriptions to four different magazines which we had liked but didn't have. Such a lot of things.

"And we will get more," Jean said shamelessly, "when we go down to Grandma's house."

This was the hired man's day off, so Bobby helped his dad with the chores while Jean helped get the necessary work done in the house, which wasn't much.

When we got down to Mother's, Grandma Butler was there already and my two older brothers Glen and Donald, and Donald's family came about the same time we did. Everett arrived from New York early Saturday morning to stay over Christmas. There were thirteen of us in all.

We had roast goose and chicken pie and all the fixin's and topped off our dinner with pineapple ice cream and cake and candy and nuts. When we were small, we never ate more than we needed, and left the rest without being tempted to overstuff. Now that we are older and supposedly grown wiser, we eat as long as we can swallow and we feel logy and uncomfortable all the rest of the day. The candy and nuts were left on the long dining table to which we could return during the afternoon whenever we had a little more room in our stomachs.

We gathered around the fragrant Christmas tree in the living room, all of us replete with food and good fellowship and let the children take the gifts from the tree and pass them around. It was sweet content, after all the weeks of hustle and bustle, to sit back quietly, with our laps so filled with gifts that they overflowed onto the floor around us. The four children used the floor entirely for their gifts, and one could hardly find a place to step through the welter of tissue paper and bright-colored wrappings, of paints and crayons and picture books and boxes. And everyone was talking at once.

We all love the bright confusion, the feeling of family solidarity. It is something to look forward to, and to hold in memory long after the day is gone.

But the children had to be at the church at seven o'clock tonight, and the barn chores had to be done before that time. Rob had to leave a little before four o'clock and Bobby went with him. Later, when the chores were done and they were back at Mother's again, Bobby told me,

"I hated to leave awfully bad and go home to help Daddy, but then I felt tired and full and dopey. It did me good to get out and work. I feel all pepped up for the evening. I hope I can sing my song well."

The program was good. The children sang well, although many of them showed the strain of a long day of revelry. They were all dressed in robes; the smaller children wore white cassocks over their long black robes. They all stood on the stage during the entire program.

Bobby's voice was never better and it soared out through the church sweet and true. After it was over he received many compliments. A music teacher who used to live in my old home town said he was especially interested in the boy soprano. He thought Bobby might have another year yet before his voice begins to change and he has to stop singing.

On our way home Bobby asked, "Could you give me any criticism on my song? Could I have sung it better some way?"

"I thought it was very good," I told him honestly.

"I want to be a singer when I grow up," he said, "and yet, I would like to be a farmer, too. I don't know which I should do."

Wednesday, December 28. Much colder and clear. The cold wave struck for fair, in regular northern style. The banshee-wind howled around the corners of the house and crept in through every exposed nook and cranny. The temperature dropped like a plummet.

The children, not minding the gale, spent several hours outdoors finishing their snow houses and snow thrones they started yesterday. The snow is ideal to model with and there is plenty of it. Bobby has a white throne built near the house which looks as comfortable as it is ornamental. It has platforms for the king's advisors and bodyguards and a wide path for the king's subjects to approach the throne. The high back of the throne is a work of art, decorated with balls of graduated sizes. Jean built a throne too, but that was used as a beheading chair and it soon caved in.

During the afternoon, the children read their Christmas books. Bobby was deep in Cooper's *The Spy*. Jean finished reading *School Days at St. Bede's* and then began *Perri*. The last book has magnificent descriptions and beautiful style. I have read parts of it twice, already.

Thursday, December 29. Eight below zero. Clear. The wind has quieted, so the cold doesn't strike in badly. There is a hard crust on the snow, and Bobby and Jean spent most of their spare time cutting blocks of the hard snow to build a regular Eskimo's hut. At least they believe it to be regular. The blocks are cut with an old bayonet blade their great-grandfather must have used in the Civil War. It makes a grand snow cutter; a much better use for a bayonet than sticking it through human flesh, to my way of thinking. It was all dull and rusty until the children used it, but now it is shiny again.

This afternoon they visited June and Stanley and had a splendid time playing with their Christmas gifts. When they got back, Jean said,

"I wish June lived nearer so I could see her more often."

"But she lives only half a mile away."

"That isn't near enough. I *like* June so much."

Saturday, December 31. Windy. Light snow falling. The work on the snow house which Bobby and Jean have been building on the little hill beside the house has gone on rapidly during the past few days, until today it was all done but the furnishings.

The blocks of snow were thin and many loads had to be drawn on the children's sleds before the house was built, even to the low entrance tunnel where the young Eskimos had to get down on their hands and knees to crawl in. They had found an old wooden door in the shop which they put on top of the snow house walls to hold the roof in place, and then covered it all with more blocks of snow. They discussed the placing of a shelf or door with as much earnestness as though the house would last for years. Last night they carried pails of water to drench the snow house so it would freeze into a hard impregnable fortress.

After everything was finished to their satisfaction, I was invited to the house-warming. It was fun crawling into the igloo. The entrance passage was carpeted with bran sacks and the igloo itself was lined with them. It was easy to mistake them for deep soft furs. There was a low table — made of snow — at one side of the room and a sacking chair stood beside it. A window in the back was covered with cardboard glass which could be easily removed to permit more light to enter.

Thus, with the new snow which has fallen today making a

soft covering over the entire house and binding up the crevices, nothing less than a thaw can destroy the structure.

"But if a thaw does come," Jean said, "we can build another one."

"And maybe we could find a way to make it better than ever before," Bobby added. "Just as this house is better than the houses we made last year. Those were silly, little-kid things but this one is good!"

So they are finding that the keenest pleasures in life lie in building. As their work is better than it was a year ago, so it ought to improve through the years, from make-believe to reality; from childhood games and problems to those of adults. But I pray to God they may never forget how to play.

The crisp, cold, sunny air smelled so fresh and good that we all felt like frolicking. When I went outdoors to call at the snow house I wore only a heavy sweater and gloves with my skirt and sweater. The sun beat down warmly. But away from the buildings the wind blew steadily. I went for a short walk up the road, and my ears were tingling and red with the cold before I got back to the house. I'll know enough to wear earmuffs next time, maybe.

The hills and valleys are beautiful but chilly. The new snow is so white and fresh that the bare trees look black by contrast, except for the white birches which are cream colored against the snow's whiteness. The tall, pointed fir trees spread green, thick branches, making colorful islands in the woods. And everywhere are the hills, rising one against the other, with narrow fertile valleys between. There is a spiritual quality in these hills which no one can gainsay.

This is the last day of the old year. I wonder what the new one has in store for us. This old year has been full of everything that is good and much which we would have liked to avoid. I'm glad we couldn't look ahead and see it all in advance.

Late tonight after the children were in bed and asleep, one of the Guernsey heifers was delivered of her first calf. Rob didn't dare leave her for long until it was over so he lay down on the couch in the living room and had short naps between his visits to the barn. When he went up at half past ten the calf had just arrived; a large fawn-colored heifer calf, nicely marked with a crescent of white in her forehead and four white socks above her feet.

Rob came back to the house and caught two pails of hot water at the faucet in the kitchen sink. He asked me to take the teakettle full of boiling water and together we went to the barn.

The young mother had been working hard for some time and she was very thirsty. She gulped down both pails of hot water, making frequent trips to her steaming new calf between drinks. She lowed softly and anxiously as she brushed her roughly with her tongue. And the little calf reached up her wet head from the bed of straw and laid it against her mother's as she was rubbed dry. Finally Rob gave the mother a big pail of hot bran mash, moistened with the water from the teakettle. All the time she was eating she kept talking to her baby softly and plaintively.

The big herd sire looked on quietly from his stout pen across the wide barn from the calving pen. He usually paces majestically up and down his pen and bellows at any strange noise, but tonight he, too, was caught up in the age-old miracle of birth, and he stared with interest at his newest offspring.

The barn was quiet late at night, with only the soft swishing noises of the cattle as they chewed their careful cuds, and the gentle lowing of the new mother. She had her calf washed and dried in the way nature intended her to do, and she was ready to rest close against her child.

We left the snug barn and went down to the house.

YANKEE • CLASSICS

IN THIS exciting new series, Yankee Books
brings back into print rare classics of
New England literature that previously
have commanded the highest prices as rare
books if and when they could be found.
The editors have selected only those titles
that are as lively and enthralling to today's
reading audience as they were to that of
a generation ago.